MEMORY

The concept of 'memory' has given rise to some of the most exciting new directions in contemporary theory.

In this much-needed guide to a burgeoning field of study, Anne Whitehead:

- presents a history of the concept of 'memory' and its uses, encompassing both memory as activity and the nature of memory
- examines debates around the term in their historical and cultural contexts
- introduces the reader to key thinkers in the field, from ancient Greece to the present day
- traces the links between theorizations and literary representations of memory

Offering a clear and succinct guide to one of the most important terms in contemporary theory, this volume is essential reading for anyone entering the field of Memory Studies, or seeking to understand current developments in Cultural and Literary Studies.

Anne Whitehead is Senior Lecturer in the School of English at Newcastle University. She is the author of *Trauma Fiction* and has edited *Theories of Memory: A Reader* and *W. G. Sebald: A Critical Companion*.

D0024221

THE NEW CRITICAL IDIOM

SERIES EDITOR: JOHN DRAKAKIS, UNIVERSITY OF STIRLING

The New Critical Idiom is an invaluable series of introductory guides to today's critical terminology. Each book:

- provides a handy, explanatory guide to the use (and abuse) of the term
- offers an original and distinctive overview by a leading literary and cultural critic
- relates the term to the larger field of cultural representation

With a strong emphasis on clarity, lively debate and the widest possible breadth of examples, *The New Critical Idiom* is an indispensable approach to key topics in literary studies.

Also available in this series:

MEMORY

Anne Whitehead

Routledge
Taylor & Francis Group

LONDON AND NEW YORK

First edition published 2009
by Routledge
2 Park Square, Milton Park, Abingdon, Oxon OX14 4RN

Simultaneously published in the USA and Canada
by Routledge
270 Madison Ave, New York, NY 10016

Reprinted 2010

Routledge is an imprint of the Taylor & Francis Group, an informa business

© 2009 Anne Whitehead

Typeset in Garamond and Scala Sans
by Taylor & Francis Books
Printed and bound in Great Britain by
TJ International Ltd, Padstow, Cornwall

British Library Cataloguing in Publication Data
A catalogue record for this book is available from the British Library

Library of Congress Cataloging-in-Publication Data
Whitehead, Anne, 1971-
Memory / Anne Whitehead. – 1st ed.
    p. cm. – (The new critical idiom)
Includes bibliographical references and index.
1. Memory. I. Title.
    BF371.W48 2008
128'.3–dc22   2008008809

ISBN 10: 0-415-40274-3   ISBN 13: 978-0-415-40274-3   (hbk)
ISBN 10: 0-415-40273-5   ISBN 13: 978-0-415-40273-6   (pbk)
ISBN 10: 0-203-88804-9   ISBN 13: 978-0-203-88804-9   (ebk)

CONTENTS

SERIES EDITOR'S PREFACE

The New Critical Idiom is a series of introductory books which seeks to extend the lexicon of literary terms, in order to address the radical changes which have taken place in the study of literature during the last decades of the twentieth century. The aim is to provide clear, well-illustrated accounts of the full range of terminology currently in use, and to evolve histories of its changing usage.

The current state of the discipline of literary studies is one where there is considerable debate concerning basic questions of terminology. This involves, among other things, the boundaries which distinguish the literary from the non-literary; the position of literature within the larger sphere of culture; the relationship between literatures of different cultures; and questions concerning the relation of literary to other cultural forms within the context of interdisciplinary studies.

It is clear that the field of literary criticism and theory is a dynamic and heterogeneous one. The present need is for individual volumes on terms which combine clarity of exposition with an adventurousness of perspective and a breadth of application. Each volume will contain as part of its apparatus some indication of the direction in which the definition of particular terms is likely to move, as well as expanding the disciplinary boundaries within which some of these terms have been traditionally contained. This will involve some re-situation of terms within the larger field of cultural representation, and will introduce examples from the area of film and the modern media in addition to examples from a variety of literary texts.

ACKNOWLEDGEMENTS

This volume was completed during a period of research leave jointly funded by Newcastle University and an Arts and Humanities Research Council (AHRC) Research Leave Award.

Particular thanks to Robert Eaglestone for his enthusiastic endorsement of the project as an external assessor for the AHRC.

I owe a tremendous debt to all of my colleagues in the School of English Literature, Language and Linguistics at Newcastle University who teach on the MA in Literary Studies: Writing, Memory Culture, and especially to those who contributed to *Theories of Memory: A Reader*. I would like to thank John Beck, Cathy Caruth and Jennifer Richards for encouraging me at the outset of the project, and Linda Anderson and Michael Rossington for generously giving their time, that most valuable of commodities, to read and comment on a draft of the volume. John Drakakis has been a judicious and supportive editor throughout. I am grateful to Mark Gillingwater for his unfailing commitment to my research obsessions, and especially for uncomplainingly visiting so many memorials and 'sites of memory' on numerous 'holidays'.

Finally, my largest gratitude goes to my students, past and present, who have helped me to think through the complexities of memory, whether on the MA in Literary Studies or on my undergraduate course Representations of the Holocaust. This volume is dedicated to them.

ABBREVIATIONS

ISLT   Marcel Proust, *In Search of Lost Time*, trans. C. K.
            Scott Moncrieff and Terence Kilmartin, rev. by D.
            J. Enright, 6 vols, London, Vintage, 2002.
RM   Pierre Nora, ed., *Realms of Memory: Rethinking the*
            French Past, English language edn, ed. and fore-
            word by Lawrence D. Kritzman, trans. Arthur
            Goldhammer, 3 vols, New York, Columbia
            University Press, 1996–98.
SE   Sigmund Freud, *The Standard Edition of the Complete*
            Psychological Works of Sigmund Freud, trans. and ed.
            by James Strachey et al., 24 vols, London,
            Vintage, 2001.

INTRODUCTION

Andreas Huyssen has recently pronounced that contemporary
Western culture is 'obsessed with the issue of memory'. At the
close of the twentieth century, he argued, memory was given
both prominence and visibility through the widespread popular-
ity of the museum, and the resurgence of the monument and the
memorial as aesthetic forms. He particularly highlighted in this
regard the inauguration of Daniel Libeskind's Jewish Museum in
Berlin, but the beginning of the twenty-first century has seen
other notable examples, most strikingly Peter Eisenman's
Memorial to the Murdered Jews of Europe, also in Berlin, and
Libeskind's controversial design of the Freedom Tower for the
rebuilding of Ground Zero in New York. For Huyssen, the contemporary memory fever is indissociable from 'the virus of amnesia that at times threatens to consume memory itself'. In
particular, he links memory's resurgence to the development of
new media technologies, which engender an accelerated form of
temporality with their instant entertainment, frenetic pace, and
quick oblivion. Cultural obsessions with memory represent what
Huyssen has termed a 'reaction formation' against such accelerated technical processes, an 'attempt to slow down information

processing' and to anchor ourselves in more extended structures of temporality (1995: 7). As such, he regards the current memory boom as a 'potentially healthy sign of contestation' against the waning of historical consciousness (1995: 9).

Huyssen's analysis of the current preoccupation with memory is valuable, but his exclusive focus on the impact of new technologies remains somewhat narrow. We can usefully supplement his work with David Lowenthal's investigation into why 'heritage' has loomed so large in Western societies over the past few decades. Lowenthal is also alert to the influence of technology, and our desire in the face of rapid and pervasive change to 'keep our bearings' (1996: 6). However, he also points to the importance of the '[m]assive migration' that has characterized the latter half of the twentieth century, and which acts to 'sharpen nostalgia' (1996: 9). Displacement is therefore countered by a quest for roots (the contemporary fascination with genealogy is especially marked among immigrant and diasporic populations) and a desire for mementoes of lifestyles that have been lost. We could add a number of further causes to those identified by Lowenthal. A renewed interest in memory followed from the popularization of discourses of virtual memory, prosthetic memory, and the electronic memory of computers. At the same time, there has been a marked rise in concern with popular memory, and a proliferation of archives, particularly oral archives, established to preserve the memories of ordinary people. Jacques Le Goff cites as exemplary in this regard the foundation of The Oral History Society at the University of Essex, which created the journal *History Workshop* and contributed to a rebirth of social and labour history (1992: 96). Finally, we could also point to the need to deal with the painful legacy of the wars, genocides, and ethnocides that have punctuated the twentieth century. In this, the Holocaust has inevitably loomed large, but there has also been a broader concern with how other traumatic instances can be remembered and lived with in the present. This has given rise not only to a multitude of public memorials and acts of commemoration, but also, notably, to the Truth Commissions of South Africa, Guatemala, Argentina, and Chile.

It is worth noting, however, that the recent surge of interest in memory has also been viewed in a less positive light by some commentators. Charles Maier has argued that the current obsession with memory, especially with the memory of the Second World War and the Holocaust, is 'a sign not of historical confidence but of a retreat from transformative politics'. For him, memory work too often takes the form of group memories contending with one another for recognition of the group's suffering, and 'reflects a new focus on narrow ethnicity' (1993: 150). Pitting memory against history, he aligns history with the desire for understanding and memory with a search for a melancholic form of emotion, which represents an 'addiction' and is potentially 'neurasthenic and disabling' (1993: 141). Kerwin Lee Klein is wary of the tendency in memory discourse to elevate memory 'to the status of a historical agent', so that 'archives remember and statues forget' (2000: 136). We should focus rather, he contends, on exactly who is doing the remembering and the forgetting. He also finds troubling the vague 'theological concepts as well as vague connotations of spirituality and authenticity' that pervade contemporary theorizing about memory (2000: 130). Like Susan Suleiman, I find such critiques salutary in foregrounding the need for continued critical self-reflection in memory studies. However, as Suleiman also notes, the recent critiques 'to some extent miss the point', for the obsession with memory, precisely because it is an obsession, 'is not something that can be made to go away' (2006: 7–8). My own critique of contemporary memory studies is located slightly differently compared with the points raised by the historians noted above. There has been a tendency in recent memory work to regard the current memory boom as unique and unprecedented, and thereby to overlook a long history of engagement with memory in the West. To this extent, memory studies have proved remarkably forgetful of their own (pre)history. This book aims to act as a corrective to such an approach, both by tracing the history of the term 'memory' in Western thought, and by locating the current memory boom as simply the latest of a series of preoccupations with memory which have punctuated Western culture.

In tracing the history of the term 'memory', I am treating it as what Mieke Bal has defined as a 'travelling concept'. Bal's use of this term is particularly pertinent for defining the aims and scope of the present volume. For Bal, then, concepts are not fixed but can travel 'between disciplines, between historical periods, and between geographically dispersed academic communities'. As they travel, their meanings change, and such modes of difference 'need to be assessed before, during and after each "trip"' (2002: 24). Although the concept of 'memory' undoubtedly travels in fascinating ways between academic disciplines and across geographical space, my intention here is limited to how it has travelled between historical periods. As I have already indicated, the travel of memory across time demonstrates that memory has a history. It is not simply the case that every culture remembers its past; as Richard Terdiman notes, 'how a culture performs and sustains this recollection is distinctive and diagnostic' (1993: 3). Memory, then, is historically conditioned; it is not simply handed down in a timeless form from generation to generation, but bears the impress or stamp of its own time and culture. This volume seeks to gain some perspective on the pervasive and ubiquitous topic of memory precisely by historicizing it; by conceiving of it as, in Terdiman's terms, *differentiated in time* (1993: 9; original emphasis). The tracing of a history of 'memory', however partial, can also point to important breaks in that tradition, moments when the meaning of the concept shifts, and a discernible difference can be registered. The organization of the volume into four distinct chapters, as outlined below, seeks to map out the main points of historical transition that seem to me the most pertinent in the Western tradition. The volume is thus divided into the following, chronologically ordered chapters: the classical, medieval, and early-modern periods; the (re)conceptualization of memory in Enlightenment and Romantic thought; the late-modern 'memory crisis' emerging out of the French Revolution and lasting to the present; and the engagement with notions of collective memory in the twentieth century.

The volume opens with a discussion of Platonic memory. I have chosen to begin at this point because it was in Plato that memory was first defined as a distinct concept. Edward Craig has thus noted that 'there is no mention of memory in the pre-Socratic fragments' (1998: 296). This is not to say that memory was unimportant prior to Plato; on the contrary, memory was, as

Edward Casey notes, 'an obsessive ... concern of the early Greeks' (1987: 11). However, memory mattered not in conceptual but in practical terms; the transmission of the rich oral culture of the Archaic period (twelfth to eighth centuries BC) depended on a trained and disciplined process of remembering. Until the introduction of alphabetic writing, the Greeks were forced to rely on the memorial powers of individuals, most notably the bards who recited epic poems such as *The Iliad* with no written texts to aid their memories. In order to perform this mnemonic feat, the bards utilized a number of mnemotechnic devices, including verbal patterns, systematic metres, and internally varying epithets. The transmission of the epic poem was so important, as Eric Havelock has pointed out, because it acted as a repository for cultural knowledge, forming 'a sort of encyclopedia of ethics, politics, history, and technology, which the effective citizen was required to learn as part of his educational equipment' (1963: 27). It was for this very reason that the bard did not simply recite the entire poem by heart, but used the mnemonic techniques as guides to composition in the present. In this way, a large part of his effort was directed to bringing the story into contact with current social conditions, preserving what was necessary for the present and transforming or discarding that which was no longer relevant.

Plato, then, represents a critical moment of transition in relation to memory. Havelock notes that in the fifth century BC, although writing skills were gradually spreading through the Greek population, there was no corresponding increase in fluent reading, which meant that an 'oral state of mind' persisted (1963: 41). Nevertheless, the impact of writing among an educated elite allowed for 'a review and rearrangement of what had ... been written down' and a corresponding 'separation of [the self] from the remembered word' (1963: 208). Havelock argues that the dialectical form, which is so intimately connected to Plato, developed from this more critical approach to the inherited tradition. Dialectic consists for Havelock in 'forc[ing] the speaker to repeat a statement already made', a rephrasing of the statement in question which was also a reviewing and an interrogation of it. Notably, although Platonic dialectic is closely bound to inscription in its origins, it does not represent a wholehearted endorsement of the written over the oral. Rather, it can be more accurately summarized as a transition from poetry to prose; through dialectic, Plato sought to replace the poeticized rhythms and language of oral memory with what Havelock terms 'an abstract language of descriptive science' (1963: 236). Deploying this more conceptual discourse in his dialogues, Plato transformed a concern to preserve and transmit the past into a search into the nature of memory itself.

Chapter 1 traces the development of the concept of memory from its Platonic origins through to the late Renaissance period. It becomes evident from this chapter that classical, medieval, and early-modern practices of remembrance were not particularly concerned with reviving past events, but rather with bringing back to mind knowledge that had been previously stored. In this sense, we can see the persistence of the oral throughout this historical period. Reviewing the development of classical theories of memory, Edward Casey has observed a 'growing secularization' of the term (1987: 14). He thus points to the attribution to memory (Mnemosyne) of divine powers in early Greek culture; for Plato, in the fifth century, memory is connected with the divine Forms but is nevertheless a knowledge that is already possessed by the individual; while in the next generation, Aristotle brings memory fully 'down to earth' by connecting it with empirical rather than divine truths (1987: 15). The 'art of memory' that emerged in Roman rhetoric, and was inherited in turn by medieval and early-modern scholars, comprised a system of mnemonics designed to aid recall, and so seemed again eminently practical in function. In Chapter 1, however, I also chart an alternative trend in memory work of this period, which witnesses a re-sacralization of the concept. This strand of thought runs from Augustine's Christian adaptation of the ancient rhetorical theory of memory, through the integration of the 'art of memory' with the Christian morality of the Middle Ages, to reach its culmination in the Neoplatonic reshaping of the 'art of memory' in the fifteenth century as a cabalistic, astrological, and magical doctrine.

In Chapter 2, I focus on Enlightenment and Romantic conceptions of memory. In this chapter, the emphasis is on the relation between memory and the self; for all of the writers discussed, memory is concerned with the personal and is inherently bound to identity. Through memory, then, the past of the individual can be revived or made actual again, in the sense of being brought into consciousness. For John Locke, this activity of reviving the past was an adjunct of reason, although for David Hume the distinction between reason and the imagination was not so clearly drawn. In the writers of the Romantic period, especially Jean-Jacques Rousseau and William Wordsworth, we can see a rich and complex literary expression of the powers of memory and the imagination to revive the past, and a reflection on the subjective vicissitudes of this activity. This period also sees a gradual shift away from memory as a conscious act of recollection or retrieval; increasing attention is focused by the Romantic writers on memories that arise by association or that come to mind entirely unbidden.

In the nineteenth century, the development of a specialized discipline of history accentuated a sense that memory was primarily subjective and concerned with the inner life. As Raphael Samuel elaborates: '[m]emory was subjective, a plaything of the emotions, indulging its caprices, wallowing in its own warmth; history, in principle at least, was objective, taking abstract reason as its guide and submitting its findings to empirical proof' (1994: ix). However, Samuel quickly goes on to contest this view of memory as history's 'negative other'; rather, he contends, the two discourses are 'dialectically related' (1994: x). Samuel's view closely accords with Richard Terdiman's elaboration of a 'memory crisis' that was precipitated by the unprecedented social, political, and technological changes of the early nineteenth century. For Terdiman, the discourses of history and memory both acted as registers of this crisis, and both therefore 'became critical preoccupations in the effort to think through what intellectuals were coming to call the "modern"' (1993: 5). Chapter 3 uses Terdiman's notion of a 'memory crisis' to frame an analysis of memory in the late-modern period, tracing an intellectual trajectory from Friedrich Nietzsche through Freud, Henri Bergson, and Marcel Proust, and into contemporary trauma theory. I argue that all of these writers are intensely concerned with a memory that has become somehow pathological, so that it seems that there is too much memory and that it threatens to overwhelm the present. The chapter seeks to emphasize that the current preoccupation with memory is indissociable from a long, late-modern 'memory crisis', and that recent new technologies, patterns of migration, and political shifts are not unique but had important, if necessarily distinct, antecedents in Western culture in the decades that followed the French Revolution.

The final chapter has some chronological overlap with Chapter 3, for it explores a different tradition, emerging in the same period, which is focused on collective remembering. Although collective memory can be seen to have origins in the work of Freud and Bergson, it reached its full expression in the writing of Maurice Halbwachs in the first half of the twentieth century. Paul Ricoeur rightly points to the 'intensely polemical situation' in the European academy at the turn of the twentieth century that pitted against each other the disciplines of sociology and psychology. In this context, individual memory and collective memory were 'placed in a position of rivalry', although the two were not as opposed as they might initially have appeared (2004: 95). In Chapter 4, I elaborate on Ricoeur's claim by addressing the different concep-tions of the scale of the 'collective' across a number of theorists, including Halbwachs, Pierre Nora, James Young, and Jay Winter. I find that there are a range of models of what constitutes the collective, which posit varying distances in the relation between the self and others. I argue that collective remembering is more effective in closely tied social groups or networks. These close relations and affective bonds, with people who count for us, operate to some extent between individual and collective memory and support Ricoeur's contention that, although the two discourses have become 'estranged from each other', they can justifiably be perceived as complementary in nature (2004: 95).

The present volume therefore offers an account of memory that emphasizes its historical vicissitudes. In so doing, my aim is to stress that memory's meaning and value transform radically in different historical periods. In this sense, as Susannah Radstone has succinctly observed, 'memory means different things at dif-ferent times' (2000: 3). Although I have invoked Bal's notion of the 'travelling concept' to articulate the process by which memory comes to differ from itself over time, we might more pertinently talk of 'memor*ies*' than of 'memory', for the concept seems at times to exceed the bounds of a singular identity. To this extent, then, we could perhaps question whether the 'art of memory', 'Romantic memory', 'traumatic memory', and 'collective memory' can indeed be encapsulated by a single concept, or whether they might be more accurately considered in terms of plurality. My chronological organization of the volume seeks to underline the important shifts in memory discourse. However, I am aware that this risks producing a narrative that, although compelling, is also problematic in certain respects. The emphasis on epochal shifts therefore risks oversimplification, while a temporal or linear account of memory is overly suggestive of notions of progress and development. In the remainder of the Introduction, I therefore want to indicate an alternative trajectory that I have sought to map out in the course of the volume. Throughout the chapters, I have traced a number of key or critical 'idioms' of memory that insistently surface and resurface in Western thought. By focusing on the key motifs around which the conceptualization of memory has been consolidated, it is possible to move away from an exclusively historical approach and to think, rather, in terms of commonalities of idiom. In what follows, I will comment briefly on the three most important motifs that are highlighted in the book, namely inscription, spatial metaphors, and 'body memory'. However, this preliminary survey is far from exhaustive and other idioms of memory can readily be discerned in the pages that follow.

In his discussion of the French word *mémoire(s)*, Jacques Derrida notes that it escapes a singular meaning and is therefore not readily translatable. Unusually, the word differs in meaning across its masculine, feminine, and plural forms. *La mémoire*, in the feminine, designates the faculty or aptitude of memory, while its plural form refers to 'memories'. The masculine, *un mémoire*, signifies a document, a report, a memorandum, and the masculine plural form can refer either to a number of such documents, or to writings that tell of a life: what we would term 'memoirs'. Derrida thus notes that in French there is discrimination between what can be said in the masculine and feminine forms, such that the masculine always implies 'a recourse to ... the written mark'

(1989: 104). Derrida's discussion signals the centrality of modes of inscription to the concept of memory. The importance of writing is evident from the very outset of this volume, for Plato's famous description of memory refers to the soul as a wax tablet which is inscribed or impressed with an image of the object to be remembered. The notion of the mind as a writing surface is remarkably consistent in the Western tradition and is evident, for example, in Roman rhetorical manuals; in Locke's metaphor of the child's mind as a blank piece of paper waiting to be inscribed; in Freud's 'Mystic Writing Pad'; and in Cathy Caruth's image of trauma indelibly engraved on the mind. In addition to inscription as metaphor, however, I have also sought to attend to the complex interrelation between oral and written forms of remembering. I have thus noted the striking persistence of oral modes of remembrance, so that throughout medieval and early-modern culture the book was an aid to recollection rather than its replacement. I have, in addition, sought to emphasize that autobiography constitutes an important art of memory, and the volume includes discussions of works by Augustine, Rousseau, Wordsworth, Proust, and Charlotte Delbo. As Derrida indicates, however, there is a discernible discrimination at work in the relation between memory and writing, so that the issue of who gets to write in the first place, and who is then subsequently absorbed into the archive, is profoundly marked by gender, as well as by class and race.

The second idiom of memory which I would like to briefly draw to attention is the metaphor of spatiality. As Edward Casey has noted, there is a strong affiliation between memory and place, for place is 'well suited to contain memories – to hold and preserve them', while memory is itself 'a place wherein the past can revive and survive' (1987: 186). Again, the importance of place was registered early in the Western tradition. Cicero thus recounts the story of Simonides, who identified the bodies of those who had been killed at a banquet by remembering where they had been seated around the table. Cicero's narrative provides a putative point of origin for the 'art of memory', a system of mnemonics that was influential from the classical to the early-modern period, and that used *loci memoriae*, memory places, in order to store remarkable amounts of information for future recall. The notion of memory as a 'storehouse' is inherited and critiqued by Locke, while Freud's topographical mapping of the mind seeks to locate precisely how and where different memories are preserved. The intersection between memory and place can also be seen in mnemonic landscape, which assumed a fundamental role, as Raphael Samuel notes, in Western Christendom of the Middle Ages, which centred on a 'far-flung network of pilgrim routes and landmarks ... conveniently sited for commemorative worship' (1994: viii). Something of the 'commemorative worship' of place can be discerned in the internalized Romantic landscapes of the mind, exemplified by Wordsworth's 'Tintern Abbey', and it can also be felt in Proust's evocations of his beloved childhood landscape of Combray. Perhaps the most notable contemporary equivalent is the hushed reverence with which we visit the sites of Holocaust memorialization, so that Europe is still marked by its network of 'pilgrim routes and landmarks', except that they now bear the names of Auschwitz, Bergen-Belsen, Treblinka. The centrality of place to collective memory was highlighted by Halbwachs, who regarded the locations in which social groups gathered as crucial to the preservation of memory, and Pierre Nora who derived the phrase *lieux de mémoire*, 'sites of memory', from Frances Yates' *loci memoriae*. Spatiality, then, is crucial to the activity of remembering, and seems as important as temporality to both its conceptualization and its practice.

The final trope of memory on which I propose to focus is 'body memory'. Although the body has been central to Western conceptions of memory, it has routinely been subordinated to consciousness and thereby overlooked. Casey observes that 'the rooting of the word "memory" in *memor* (mindful) and ultimately of "remembering", "reminding", and "reminiscing" in *mens* (mind)' indicate the bias towards mental processes of remembering in the very etymology of the language that we use (1987: 258). However, Mary Warnock rightly notes that 'memory and the state of the body, and especially of the brain, are ... closely linked' (1987: 2). Aristotle was the first to note the physical basis of remembering, which had been overlooked by Plato, and his emphasis on the importance of the visual image resulted in a similar stress on visualization in the 'art of memory'. Wordsworth's poetry continued to place an overwhelming emphasis on the role of the visual in the memory process; 'Tintern Abbey', for example, documents a detailed comparison between the landscape that the speaker sees in the present and the remembered landscape that he saw five years previously. For Proust, however, memory's sensual basis lies elsewhere; his famous involuntary memory sequences respond to the senses of taste, touch, hearing, and smell, but notably not to sight. Charlotte Delbo's description of the traumatic memory of Auschwitz likewise focuses on taste and smell in preference to the visual. The role of the physical in remembering comprises one form of 'body memory', but Bergson also alerts us to the importance of habit, which comprises the body's own form or mode of remembrance. As Edward Craig has pointed out, amnesia provides a dramatic demonstration of the efficacy of habit, in exposing 'the difference between memory as retention of language and skills, and memory as the power to recollect and to recognize specific things' (1998: 296). In amnesia, then, we lose our recall of facts but retain our general power of retention. Although Bergson himself regarded habit memory with some disparagement, I argue in Chapter 4 that it subsequently became important in theories of collective memory for conceptualizing commemorative rituals and practices. I also highlight, finally, another form of 'body memory', with which Bergson's contemporary Freud was intensely concerned, namely traumatic memory. From Freud's analysis of hysterical symptoms to the intensely physical memories of Auschwitz described by Delbo, it is evident that the body plays an important, if still contested, role in traumatic forms of remembering.

In tracing memory from antiquity to modernity, the present volume moves between philosophical and literary texts. I regard both discursive modes as important to the theorization of memory, and seek to demonstrate that memory's history is as firmly embedded in Augustine, Wordsworth, and Proust as in Plato, Freud, or Bergson. Indeed, rich and suggestive areas of dialogue can be discerned between the literary and the philosophical as, for example, between Hume and Wordsworth, or between Bergson and Proust. It is, however, notable that across both discursive fields the predominant voices of memory are male. Anna Reading has noted that, although in the classical world memory and history were represented by the goddesses Mnemosyne and Clio respectively, these female icons were far from 'indicative of the value of women and men or the authority given to their articulations of the past' (2002: 8). Likewise, in Plato's conjecture that recollection revived knowledge acquired in a life before birth, the role of women, those responsible for bringing the child into the world and giving it foundational knowledge, was elided (Craig 1998: 296–7). Marianne Hirsch and Valerie Smith have recently suggested that this is one area of memory discourse that has remained consistent over time. 'What a culture remembers and what it chooses to forget', they argue, 'are intricately bound up with issues of power and hegemony, and thus with gender' (2002: 6). Public media and official archives memorialize the experiences of the powerful and it has therefore been necessary to turn to alternative archives, such as the oral testimony archives noted above, to hear the voices of women and other disenfranchised groups. A number of recent publications have aimed at opening up the question of memory and gender (see, for example, Sturken 1997; Haaken 1998; Kuhn 2002; Reading 2002; Leydersdorff et al. 2005; and Chedgzoy 2007). However, as Reading reflects, none of the recent memory classics, including Halbwachs' *The Collective Memory*, Nora's *Realms of Memory*, or Young's *Texture of Memory*, have 'address[ed] gender issues' (2002: 15). In reading this volume, it is therefore necessary to remain attentive to who is doing the writing, and whose remembering has been absorbed into the canon. This makes evident the relative degrees of power and powerlessness, privilege, and disenfranchisement that have shaped dominant memory discourse.

The preceding paragraph makes clear that a history of memory is also necessarily a history of forgetting. For the early Greeks, as Edward Casey remarks, remembering and forgetting were intimately intertwined: 'they [were] given explicit mythical representation in the coeval figures of Lemosyne and Mnemosyne, who are conceived as equals *requiring* each other' (1987: 12; original emphasis). This volume traces, then, a parallel history of the concept of forgetting, which can also be seen to shift in meaning and significance across different historical periods. In the classical 'art of memory', based on a system of storage and retrieval, for-getting registered only as a fault in the mnemonic system. Not theorized in and of itself, it marked a point of failure or break-down, whether in the psychic apparatus or in the image of the object to be remembered. For the Enlightenment philosophers, for whom memory was coeval with the self, forgetting in the form of amnesia or periods of unconsciousness such as sleep, troubled their conceptions and became a point of obsessive return. It was with the nineteenth-century 'crisis of memory', however, that forgetting took on its own significance. For Freud, forgetting was conceived as a blocked or overcathected memory, while for Proust a period of forgetting necessarily preceded the miraculous resur-rection of involuntary remembrance. Harald Weinrich registers this crucial shift through a semantic discussion of the Greek word *aletheia*, 'truth'. He observes that the word combines the negative prefix '*a-*' with the component '*-leth*', which also occurs in the name of Lethe, the river of forgetting. From this, he argues, 'one can ... conceive truth as the "unforgotten" or the "not-to-be-for-gotten"'. Weinrich's analysis accords with the value placed on remembering over forgetting in earlier Western thought. However, as Weinrich goes on to acknowledge, in modern times we have 'grant[ed] forgetting a certain truth as well' (2004: 4). The present volume concludes, then, by assessing the contemporary significance of forgetting. I argue that, in the context of the col-lective, a degree of forgetting is as important as remembering for allowing the community to function in the aftermath of social and historical catastrophes. Although this volume is titled *Memory*, I am therefore also increasingly preoccupied with the question of forgetting. This concept not only forms the shadowy underside of memory but, more precisely, shapes and defines the very contours of what is recalled and preserved; what is transmitted as remem-brance from one generation to the next; and what is thereby handed down to us, in our turn, to cherish or discard, but above all to reflect critically upon.

1

MEMORY AND INSCRIPTION

THE WAX TABLET

This chapter will look at some of the texts from the classical and early-modern periods which helped to construct the dominant discourse of memory in the West. These texts posit an inextricable connection between memory and the means used to record that memory. From the very outset, then, remembering is intimately bound to figures of writing and inscription.

The most obvious starting point is Plato's description of memory in the *Theaetetus* (c. 360 BC), which established an important and influential model for later thinkers. This text comprises a dialogue between Socrates (an Athenian philosopher), Theodorus (a mathematician), and Theaetetus (a young aristocrat), which is concerned with the nature of knowledge and the difference between knowledge and perception. In seeking to distinguish between thought and perception, Socrates explains that objects of perception are a succession of constantly changing awarenesses, whereas objects of thought are those objects of perception to which we have given some degree of stability by imprinting them on the mind. In order to explain further, Socrates asks Theaetetus to imagine that the mind contains a block of wax. When we wish to convert an object of perception into an object of thought, we hold this wax under the perception and imprint it, stamping the mind with an impression of the object as with a seal ring. We remember and know what has been imprinted for as long as the impression of it remains.

Plato's model of the wax tablet introduces into the discourse of memory a series of distinct, if related, questions. First, memory seems to have both active and passive components. For Socrates, the act of remembering is primarily active: it is when we 'want to remember' that we 'subject the block to the perception or the idea and stamp the impression into it' (1987: 99–100). However, as Paul Ricoeur points out, the notion of the imprint also involves 'the external causality of an impetus … which is itself at the origin of pressing the seal into the wax' (2004: 51). Memory, then, seems to be uncertainly suspended between that which we wish to retain, making a conscious effort to do so, and that which impresses itself upon us so that it is more passively experienced or undergone.

The second question which arises is that of the truth of memory. How is it possible to know whether what we remember in the present corresponds with what we once perceived? Plato makes clear that error can be caused either by the erasing of the marks on the wax or by matching the wrong imprint with a present perception, an error akin to that of someone placing his feet in the wrong footprints. Socrates explains to Theaetetus that the wax tablet in our minds is of varying and uneven quality in different individuals. Some people are fortunate and have a wax that is smooth and of the right consistency, so that impressions are clear, deep, and lasting. These individuals are quick to learn and also have good memories. For others, however, the wax is too soft, so that the impressions are indistinct and easily blurred: these people are quick to learn but forgetful. If the wax is too hard, however, it is difficult to make an impression but, once there, it is lasting: individuals with these types of minds are slow to learn but retain memories well. The problem of forgetting is thus posed in the first instance as an effacement of traces, either because they are unclear at the moment of imprinting or insufficiently deep. It is then re-posed as a defect in adjusting the present image to the imprint. This may again arise from the quality of the wax, which means that the images are indistinct. The wax tablets also differ in size from one person to another: if impressions are crowded together in a small mind, they are more likely to become blurred and confused. In either case, people are unable to assign what they hear or see or think quickly to the proper impression; they are slow-witted and hold false or erroneous beliefs. In introducing the model of the wax tablet, on which marks were temporary and could be easily erased, Plato was thus as intimately concerned with the nature of forgetting as with the nature of remembering.

The final question which is posed by Plato's metaphor of the wax tablet is the physical nature of the images that are inscribed. Plato's model of the memory process implies that the images or objects of thought are to some degree material: they are stamped or incised into matter and are stored there so that they can be available for subsequent recall. Later writers, including Aristotle, were highly attentive to the physical or sensory foundations of remembering. Plato, too, initially seems to be interested in questions of materiality, in his extended discussion of the physical variations of different minds and their resulting capacity for storing and recalling images. However, his metaphor is notably distinct from the later Aristotelian model. Unlike Aristotle, Plato believes that there is a knowledge that is not derived from sense impressions. For Plato, there are latent in our minds the forms or impressions of the Ideas, the realities which the soul knew before its descent into the body. True knowledge, then, consists of matching sense impressions onto the imprint of the higher reality of which physical forms are mere reflections. In a complex dialectic of remembering and forgetting, Plato posits a three-stage process in which the pre-birth glimpse of the Ideas is succeeded by birth, a forgetting of what was previously seen. The soul enters at birth into oblivion and is covered with a layer of wax on which there is as yet no impression. However, it seems that the wax tablet is not completely wiped clean: there remain imprints of the Ideas, so that we retain a latent knowledge of them. Central to Plato's philosophy is that knowledge of the truth consists in remembering or recollecting the Ideas which were once seen by the soul. All knowledge and all learning is thus an act of remembering, an attempt to recollect these realities. The knowledge with which memory is concerned is thus of a very specific and distinct type. Plato is not concerned with individual facts and events nor a personal, subjective memory. Although he recognizes that we have the capacity to preserve sensibly experienced memories, he is primarily interested in an immaterial, impersonal reality, which is not tied to the concrete world of things and so is unchanging and eternal.

For Plato, the only route to knowledge of the Ideas or eternal realities is through dialectical enquiry. Plato believes that there are two distinct kinds of learning. The learner can simply absorb information transmitted from a teacher or, alternatively, the learner can work things out for himself. Dialectics conforms to the second kind of learning. In a process of repeated questioning, the learner has to decide the right answer to the questions posed. In this way, he works out an explanation for understanding why something is true, rather than relying on opinion, received information or trust. The standard subjects of dialectical enquiry are directly linked to the higher reality of the Ideas, encompassing such topics as the Equal, the Greater and the Less, the Beautiful, the Good, the Just, and the Holy. Recollection is integral to the dialectical process because the conduct of the discussion requires the participants to recollect relevant data. However, as Richard Sorabji points out, dialectical discussion is not only accompanied by but also culminates in recollection. Through questioning, the learner uncovers in himself the knowledge that is latent in him. Knowledge is thus derived not from the external world, or from someone else, but from within oneself. Richard Sorabji observes:

> For if we acquire knowledge of these things by a process of recollection, this fact can be used to argue for the discarnate existence of the soul before birth. For our ability to recollect these things implies our prior knowledge of them. And the only available time in which we can have acquired such prior knowledge, it is argued, is the time before birth.
>
> (1972: 36)

Recollection is also integral to the dialectical process because it works analogously to it. Just as dialectical reasoning involves a succession of closely associated steps, so for Plato the process of recollection involves an association between ordinary things in this world and the Ideas in the world above.

Plato's fullest demonstration of the importance of recollection to dialectical enquiry is in his *Meno* (c. 387 BC). In conversation with Socrates, Meno (a young aristocrat) argues that one can never find out anything new: either one knows it already, in which case there is no need to find it out, or else one does not, and in that case one would not be able to recognize it when it was found. As a way out of this either/or dilemma, Socrates proposes the idea that knowledge is recollection, which recognizes that we can know something in an imperfectly conscious way, so that it is both known and not known at the same time. He argues that in this life, it is possible to start from something that we consciously know, and by a process of association, be reminded of all the rest of the knowledge that is latent in our minds. In demonstration of this, Socrates shows that Meno's uneducated slave boy implicitly knows the truths of geometry and can recollect them merely by being asked the right questions. Socrates insists no less than four times that he is not teaching the boy, but simply posing questions to him. In responding, the slave boy reasons out the principles of geometry, and Socrates concludes that 'the spontaneous recovery of knowledge that is in him is recollection' (1956: 138). Although at present the boy's knowledge, newly awakened, has a provisional or tentative quality, Socrates argues that if the same questions are put to him on many occasions and in different ways, he will have as firm a grasp of geometry as anybody else. It is worth noting, however, that the slave boy would not have 'recovered' the principles of geometry without skilful prompting by Socrates: although the latter claims that he is not teaching, it seems that the boy's knowledge comes as much from without as from within, so that Plato's dichotomy of internal/external is not as straightforward as it at first appears.

For Plato, then, memory is an art that is inherently dialectical, enacted through an oral question-and-answer process. The medium of speech is privileged because it offers both immediate connection and the intimate understanding that can come from prolonged personal contact. Confusions and misunderstandings can be uncovered and cleared up in the questioning process, and the type or form of speech can be varied according to the needs of the learner. In contrast, Plato reveals a marked distrust of writing, arguing that it will lead individuals to rely on external letters and signs, and to lose the ability to recollect that which is within. This view was most forcefully articulated in Plato's *Phaedrus* (c. 370 BC), a conversation between Socrates and Phaedrus, an upper-class Athenian who is a devotee of the new rhetorical learning. Socrates is critical of rhetoric and seeks to establish dialectic as the true art of speaking. In order to do this, Socrates tells Phaedrus a story which is precisely concerned to elucidate the value of speech over writing in relation to the activity of remembering.

Socrates' story relates how the Egyptian god Theuth, who invented number and calculation, geometry and astronomy, also discovered writing. He presented this new branch of expertise to the Egyptian king Thamus, suggesting that it should be spread throughout the land. When asked by Thamus to elaborate on the advantages and disadvantages of writing, Theuth replied: 'But *this* study, King Thamus, will make Egyptians wiser and improve their memory; what I have discovered is an elixir of memory and wisdom' (Plato 2005: 62; original emphasis). Thamus, however, argued that it would have precisely the opposite effect. Writing would atrophy memory, because rather than trusting on their inner resources, individuals would rely on external marks made by others. Writing could act as a prompt for recollection, but not as an aid for true remembering. Thamus also contended that writing could not respond to questioning nor could it defend itself against contradiction or argument; it gives the appearance of intelligence but is not concerned with true explanation. As Jack Goody and Ian Watt have pointed out, Socrates delivers his attack on writing in the form of a fable or myth, 'a distinctively oral ... mode of discourse' (1968: 50). Although they warn that it would be wrong to represent Plato as a wholehearted protagonist of the oral tradition, they nevertheless state:

> Plato considered the transmission of the cultural tradition was more effective and permanent under oral conditions, at least as regards the individual's initiation into the world of essential values.
>
> (Goody and Watt 1968: 51)

It is also the case, however, that Plato communicates his predominantly oral story in writing, within the context of the dialogue. Arguably for him the highest form of communication is that of living dialectic in speech, but the next best thing is the written dialogue form which, in posing questions rather than giving answers and in evoking the rhythms and forms of speech, responds to at least some of Thamus' criticisms.

Plato, then, opposes speech and writing in the *Phaedrus* and privileges the former over the latter. However, as Jacques Derrida has eloquently argued in 'Plato's Pharmacy', there is a further opposition at play in Plato's work, which precisely contrasts 'good' and 'bad' writing. 'Bad' writing is the script of texts, a form of writing which is opposed in the *Phaedrus*. As Socrates makes clear in the dialogue, this writing is resolutely external; it is a supplement, an appendage, and as such is mechanical and lifeless. In Plato, however, as we have seen, writing also insinuates itself as metaphor into the act of true remembering. 'Good' writing describes the act of inscription outlined in the *Theaetetus*, the impressions that are stamped or inscribed into the wax of the soul. Plato seeks to emphasize that these 'written' marks or traces are entirely internal, spontaneous; independent of external agency or control. Plato's philosophy is marked for Derrida, then, by a kind of 'dream', a fantasy that the 'good' scripture of remembering can be distilled or separated from the 'bad' script of texts. Writing as text is expelled from the soul, and remembrance is accordingly interiorized. The problem, as Derrida points out, is that a principle of contamination is nevertheless at work. Plato would seek to separate the oppositions internal–external, natural–artificial, essential–supplementary, eternal–contingent, living–dead. However, writing repeatedly resists his own intention, so that the inside is invaded or intruded upon by the outside. Derrida observes: 'The outside is already *within* the work of memory' (1981: 109). In order to recall that which is not present, memory needs signs and so is always already contaminated by the signifier, the surrogate, the supplement.

For Derrida, the word *pharmakon* acts in Plato's text to embody this principle of resistance or contamination. In classical Greek *pharmakon* takes on a double meaning, for it signifies both remedy and poison. When Theuth presents the invention of writing to Thamus, he describes it as a *pharmakon*, an 'elixir' or remedy for memory. Thamus' response makes clear, however, that Theuth is deceiving either himself or the king in giving only one side of the story, and repressing the alternative signification. Thamus accordingly elaborates the different ways in which writing is a poison. Derrida points out that the overdetermination of the word marks a problem for translators, who in fixing its meaning as either 'remedy' or 'poison' inevitably skew our reading of the text. However, for Derrida this is a problem which does not arise by chance but is rather characteristic of Plato's discourse. In Plato, the same word will often take on alternative meanings and significations at different places in the text, according to its context. It is characteristic of Plato himself to neutralize this textual play, to attempt to master ambiguity by inserting simple, clear-cut oppositions. According to the logic of the *Phaedrus*, then, the *pharmakon* is passed off (by Theuth) as a helpful remedy, whereas it is in truth harmful. For Derrida, Plato's most lasting legacy to the tradition of Western philosophy is to determine signification within the play of thematic oppositions. Plato, in particular, inaugurated an opposition between 'good' and 'bad' forms of writing, which acted to relegate script to a subordinate and subservient position. Derrida is, in turn, concerned to read Plato against the grain, in order to demonstrate that textuality is constituted by differences and that it is by nature both heterogeneous and excessive.

As a model for thinking about memory, Plato has exerted a powerful influence over the Western tradition. His opposition to writing can be traced in a lasting and persistent distrust of the archive as constituted by written records, in contrast to living memory. In Chapter 4 I will accordingly consider whether the written form of the archive constitutes, for a writer such as Pierre Nora, more of a 'poison' than a 'remedy'. Through the metaphor of the image that is imprinted, Plato also places emphasis, as Paul Ricoeur has pointed out, on 'the presence of an absent thing' and so is not explicitly concerned with 'the reference to past time' (2004: 6). The 'marks' to which memory is attached are absent forms which are implicitly anterior, but Plato does not reflect on this at any length. Rather, he is concerned to turn memory into myth by connecting it with a prenatal knowledge, which entails the relearning of that which was forgotten at birth. Plato's emphasis on immaterial forms, the Ideas, exerted a particularly strong influence on the Christian Latin West through the writings of Augustine. Platonic Idealism also influenced the development of Renaissance Platonism, as will be discussed in the next section. Plato's writing on memory was, however, only one of two rival and complementary discourses to emerge out of Socratic philosophy. The second was advanced by Plato's student Aristotle (384–322 BC), who set out his ideas in the brief text *De memoria et reminiscentia* [Of Memory and Recollection] (350 BC). It is to this work that I will turn for the remainder of this section, in order to explore the ways in which Aristotle both extends and breaks with the Platonic model of remembering.

Aristotle inherits in his writing Plato's model of the wax tablet. Douwe Draaisma points out, however, that Aristotle 'gives the metaphor ... which in Plato is still a playful image, a more literal meaning' (2000: 25). For Aristotle, who is more influenced than Plato by the empirical notion that knowledge comes through the senses, the material forms of external things are somehow impressed upon the receiving sense organ. In a secondary process, which takes place when perception is over, the sense image is then transferred into the soul in order to provide a vehicle for remembering and thinking. There is, then, a distinction between sense images and memory images; the latter are produced or derived from the former by a kind of secondary imprinting process. For Aristotle, memory necessarily contains images of what has entered through the senses; he does not believe, like Plato, that the objects of thought can exist separately from the sensible, material world. Aristotelian memory is a physical process, during which, as Draaisma notes: '[s]omething is literally stamped into the body, an impression with physiological features, a material trace' (2000: 25).

Aristotle focuses on the connection between the body and the soul, in contrast to Plato's *Theaetetus* where attention is quickly diverted from the imprinting of objects of perception to the imprinting of the soul with the divine Ideas. From this basis he goes on to elaborate why some individuals have a disposition to remember, while in others the faculty is weak. Initially, this recalls Plato's discussion of the various types and qualities of wax. Aristotle points out that memory is weak in those who are either very quick or very slow; in the former, the wax is too fluid and so the image does not remain, while in the latter the wax is too hard and so the image does not take hold. However, Aristotle goes beyond Plato in attributing poor memory to medico-physical causes. Thus he points out that the imprint of the image is neither clearly nor distinctly impressed if the soul is 'subject to a lot of movement'. This can be caused either by illness ('some trouble') or by the age of the person concerned. In both the very young and the very old, memory is weak because the individual is 'in a state of flux', either because he is growing or because he is wasting away. For these people, then, the changes that are taking place within them make it as if 'the seal were falling on running water' (Aristotle 1972: 50). The memory image is for Aristotle intimately linked to the physical, although Richard Sorabji cautions that it cannot be entirely reduced to this level. He observes of Aristotle: 'The memory image is a physiological affection, in some sense of "is" analogous to that in which a house is bricks. But it is not "simply" this' (Sorabji 1972: 16).

Aristotle is also concerned with the question of what makes a memory image distinct from an image in the imagination. In response, he points out unequivocally, memory is 'of the past' (Aristotle 1972: 48). It thus contrasts with perception which is of the present, and prediction which is of the future. Whenever an individual remembers, the image is accompanied in the soul by the awareness that one has heard, or perceived, or thought this before. It is thus distinct from an imagined image because one recognizes it from the past. Second, the remembered image is a true copy of something. Aristotle's two-stage model of impression, which transforms the object perceived into a sense image and then into a memory image, posits a causal link between the physical object and one's present mental image of it. One's memory image of a scene is thus for Aristotle a copy of that scene, although he sometimes seems to imply that the memory image is a copy of one's view or perception of that scene rather than what was necessarily there. The memory image, then, is derived from a past (object of) perception and it necessarily represents a likeness of that which is remembered. This point, as Sorabji notes, marks a distinct difference between Aristotle and later mnemonic systems, for the images in these systems often symbolize the objects remembered and are indeed very unlike them. Mnemonic systems, Sorabji points out, tend to operate with 'images *for*, rather than ... images *of*, what is remembered' (1972: 3; original emphasis).

Aristotle's notion of the memory image as a copy or likeness leads him into a further question. How, while perceiving an image, can we simultaneously remember something distinct from it, namely the thing that it represents? How, in other words, do we remember that which we no longer perceive at the same time as we perceive the memory image? Aristotle answers this by turning to a metaphor of inscription. He cites the example of a figure drawn on a panel, which can be seen both as something to be contemplated in its own right and as a copy of another thing. So with the memory image, we can view it both in and of itself or in relation to an object earlier perceived. Although Aristotle seems confident that we can clearly distinguish the remembered from the imagined image, there is here a notable equivocation in his account. If the memory image is both autonomous (like the imagined image) and bears a relation to an original, there seems to be a degree of ambiguity in finally distinguishing between memory and the imagination.

I have so far elaborated that part of Aristotle's account of memory which emphasizes memory as a fundamentally passive process. The second half of his treatise is concerned, however, to distinguish memory from recollection, which comprises the active and deliberate search for a memory. This is a much more intellectual endeavour and is more akin to Plato's account of memory, which was concerned with recollecting the Ideal forms that we encountered before birth. For Aristotle, though, recollection as a process of reasoning is concerned to recover something that one has previously learned or experienced in this life. Aristotle also seems to disagree with Plato's emphasis on dialectical questioning, in which the process of recollection inevitably involves somebody else. For Aristotle, by contrast, recollection is an autonomous, independent, and self-motivated search.

In his account of recollection, Aristotle stresses the need for a methodological basis to the search. First, it is important to note that recollection works by laws of association: we are reminded of something by that which is similar, opposite, or neighbouring to it. The act of recollection, then, involves moving through a series of memory images that are related in an order of succession by locating a suitable starting point and exciting a physiological change which will pass from one image to another until it reaches the object of the search. The problem with this model is that several paths remain open from a single starting point: the quest can easily take a wrong track so that there is no guarantee of success. Pathways of association can therefore be strengthened by repetition, which helps to maintain them and to keep them open. Here, then, Aristotle emphasizes the importance of habit in facilitating the process of recollection. He also recommends grouping memory images in sequences of three, looking at the middle element of the triad, and then moving on along the chain. This acts as a form of shorthand, so that the individual can pass rapidly along a chain of associations in order to locate the desired image. Implicit here is the importance of storing that which is to be remembered in an orderly sequence from the outset. Although Aristotle does not elaborate on the examples that he gives, so that they remain somewhat obscure and indecipherable to the modern reader, they nevertheless provide indications that number and alphabet are seen to be useful both in terms of organizing or storing memory images and for conceptualizing the process of recollection.

Aristotle's writing on recollection contributes to, and is inseparable from, the dialectical tradition inherited from Plato. Dialectical debating, as Aristotle taught it, was a development from earlier forms. Richard Sorabji outlines the typical Aristotelian debate as follows:

> [O]ne person, the answerer, would be required to defend a certain thesis. His opponent, the questioner, would try to make him admit the negation of that thesis. He would do so by putting questions in a form that called for a 'yes' or 'no' answer. With certain exceptions, other forms of question and answer were not allowed.
>
> (Sorabji 1972: 27)

Aristotle was highly critical of the training in dialectical debate provided by many of his predecessors, who had offered their students ready-made arguments that were simply to be memorized (this practice is also attacked by Plato in his *Phaedrus*, for it represents learning without understanding). Aristotle is not opposed to his students memorizing, but he is concerned that they should memorize general patterns of argument and the theses of various schools. They then have them ready to hand and can deploy them in the course of a debate, without being wholly reliant on them. Aristotle's writing, then, suggests that memorizing was important for students of dialectic as a means of preparing themselves for debates. Recollection can, for Aristotle, be useful in dialectical argument but it is not, as for Plato, an inherently dialectical process. In the effort to recollect, Aristotle emphasizes the principles of order and association and also the role of visualization. Aristotle's writing on recollection was subsequently subsumed into the tradition of the 'art of memory', to be discussed in the next section, and read as a kind of memory treatise. Aristotle was used, as Frances Yates explains, to provide 'philosophical justification for the artificial memory' (1966: 49). It is important, however, to separate Aristotle from later appropriations of his work. Aristotle contributes to the discourse of memory an insistence that we ground our understanding of remembering in the physical realm, and he also naturalizes the process of recollection, bringing it closer to our everyday experience. His writing departs from Plato but also builds on his insights, emphasizing recollection as a recovery of what had earlier been seen or encountered, and as a process in which searching does not necessarily lead to finding. He also, like Plato, highlights the partiality of memory. Whether the memory has been stamped by divine Ideas or whether it is impressed with images derived from sensory objects, part of the original experience is, as Mary Carruthers observes, 'inevitably lost or "forgotten"' in the process (1990: 25).

THE ART OF MEMORY

In 1968, the psychologist A. R. Luria published his renowned study of the Russian mnemonist Shereshevskii, referred to by Luria simply as S., who had a remarkable capacity for remembering facts and numbers, even after many years had elapsed. As Luria relates, S. possessed a natural gift for recall which was enhanced by training. Entirely self-taught, he devised a system in which he fixed a particular place in his mind – S. used Gorky Street in Moscow – and deposited there images of what he wished to recall. In the act of recollection, he mentally walked through the place retrieving the images from where he had left them. On the rare occasions when S. 'forgot' an element in a series, Luria observes that this was a fault of perception rather than of recall. S. had simply failed to 'see' an image because he had placed it in a bad location. He solved such problems by inserting a streetlamp into his memorized scene for illumination or by adding in a contrasting background. Although S. was not formally trained in mnemonics, the system that Luria describes bears remarkable similarities to the 'art of memory' elaborated by Roman writers. In what follows, I will therefore elaborate on the process of memorization as it developed in the context of the classical rhetorical tradition.

In ancient Rome, memorization was raised to the level of an 'art', a technique to be learned and mastered. This art belonged to rhetoric and was primarily a means by which the orator could improve his memory and deliver long speeches with accuracy. The memory was a storehouse of topics on themes such as 'justice', 'temperance', or 'fortitude', on which the orator could draw in order to fit words to the present occasion. Memory was regarded as the fifth part of rhetoric, which comprised invention (the discovery of something to say); arrangement (the organization of what had been found); style (the ornamentation through words and figures); delivery (the performance of the speech, including elements such as gesture and diction); and memory (consigning the speech to memory). There are three main ancient sources that describe the 'art of memory': the *Rhetorica ad Herennium* [Rhetoric to Herennius], written by an anonymous teacher of rhetoric in Rome between 86 and 82 BC, but wrongly attributed to Cicero in the Middle Ages; Cicero's own *De oratore* [On the Ideal Orator] (55 BC); and Quintilian's *Institutio oratoria* [The Method of Oratory] (written at the end of the first century BC). Together, these texts develop the art of Greek mnemonics (of which no extant texts survive) and resituate memory from the context of dialectics to that of rhetoric.

The *Ad Herennium* is the only full treatise on the 'art of memory' in Latin to survive. The anonymous author distinguishes in the first instance between natural and artificial memory, and makes clear that his interest is in the latter. He then goes on to elaborate the 'place system' in which the individual memorizes a set of places, for example a street or a building with a series of rooms, which act as background images. Onto this background are then placed a second set of images which symbolize what is to be remembered, for example the points of a speech. In recollecting, the individual runs through the set of places in his mind in order to find the image required. The 'art of memory' is thus concerned not with remembering past experiences but with storing away what has been learned for future recall. Proof of a good memory lies not simply in the capacity to recall information quickly but in the ability to move about memory with confidence and ease, which demonstrates true understanding of the material rather than simple rote learning.

The *Ad Herennium* gives a series of rules for backgrounds, which should be conspicuous; not too crowded; of moderate size; not too dimly or too brightly lit, and not too close or too far away. In each instance, the emphasis is on putting in place a background against which the images can be clearly and distinctly perceived. The author suggests placing an image on every fifth or tenth place, in order to make it easier to move around the series. He then elaborates rules for the creation of images, which should be abbreviated symbols of what is to be remembered, rather than likenesses or copies as in Aristotle. The images should not be too numerous and they must be carefully delineated. They should also be striking or singular in some way – violent, active, beautiful, ugly, comic, or obscene – evoking an emotional response in order to be more memorable. The author is opposed to 'ready-made' images, arguing that each person should find or make his own associations. In outlining the relation of backgrounds and images, the author makes clear that he is talking about a process of inscription. The background is equivalent to a wax tablet which can be wiped clean in order for new images to be inscribed. The arrangement of the images on the background is a form of inner writing. Remembering or recollecting is analogous to reading what has been written. Successful remembering depends, as in Plato and Aristotle, on having a good, clean surface, in this instance a well-ordered background and clearly inscribed figures or images.

The *Ad Herennium* also distinguishes between remembering 'things' and remembering 'words'. Both kinds of memory use the place system and, in each instance, recollection is achieved by association, using consciously selected visual images. The author admits, however, that the system is more effective for remembering things than for remembering words. Word-for-word memorization in this fashion is cumbersome and he indicates that exact memorization of short passages is better achieved by repeating the words two or three times to fix them in the memory before attaching images to them. Similarly, Luria relates that S. found his place system worked better with series of objects or numbers than with extended passages of text. He found it burdensome to break the words down into units of sound and find associated visual images for each. The author of *Ad Herennium* concludes that memory for words using the place system should be tackled because it is more difficult than memory for things, rather than for its own intrinsic merit or value.

Cicero's *De oratore* presents the rules for memory in a condensed form, as the author presumes that his reader is already familiar with works such as *Ad Herennium*. Cicero treats of the five parts of rhetoric in an elegant, discursive manner, although he alters the conventional order, placing memory third in the series, so that it comes after arrangement but before style. Speculating on this reordering, James M. May and Jakob Wisse argue that Cicero may be avoiding the suggestion, implied by the usual positioning of 'memory' after 'delivery', that one should memorize the exact words of the speech rather than the overall content and structure (2001: 37). The subject of memory is introduced by Cicero with the story of Simonides. For Cicero, and later for Quintilian, Simonides of Ceos stands as the originator of the 'art of memory'. As Antonius, the speaker of the second book of *De oratore*, who was renowned for his excellent memory, relates, Simonides had just left a banqueting hall when it collapsed, killing those who remained within. Simonides was able to identify all of the dead by recalling where each guest was seated at the table. For Cicero, the most important point about this anecdote is its demonstration that memory is fundamentally spatial: it works on an orderly arrangement of places. Cicero also notes, although this point was not subsequently taken up by Quintilian in his discussion of the story, that memory is essentially visual. Antonius argues that sight is the keenest of our senses and we should accordingly make visual that which we wish to remember, converting it into an image or figure. In the story of Simonides, then, the two main principles of mnemonics are established: the remembrance of images and the importance of order.

In *De oratore*, Cicero also deploys the image of memory as writing. Like the author of *Ad Herennium*, he argues that in the place system the background acts as a wax tablet on which we inscribe signs or images. Antonius thus observes that 'the order of the localities would preserve the order of the things, while the images would represent the things themselves; and we would use the localities like a wax tablet, and the representations like the letters written on it' (Cicero 2001: 219). Mary Carruthers has rightly commented on the remarkable persistence of the imagery of inscription to describe the memory process, observing: '[e]ven the most apparently pictorial of mnemonic systems are based on principles governing the nature of signs rather than on iterative copying' (1990: 28). In the place system, metaphors of inscription coexist with but are not superseded by architectural imagery, so that memory remains in conception a process of writing and of reading.

Quintilian's *Institutio oratoria* offers one of the clearest descriptions of the mnemonic place system. Taking the example of a building as background, Quintilian recommends that we should fix in our minds not only all of the rooms but also the ornaments and furniture with which the rooms are decorated. Images are 'entrusted not merely to bedrooms and parlours, but even to the care of statues and the like' (1979: 223). As Frances Yates points out, Quintilian makes clear that in conceptualizing the process of memorization '[w]e have to think of the ancient orator as moving in imagination through his memory building *whilst* he is making his speech, drawing from the memorized places the images he has placed on them' (1966: 18; original emphasis). Like Cicero, Quintilian also aligns the place system to the metaphor of the wax tablet, confirming that 'certain impressions are made upon the mind, analogous to those which a signet-ring makes on wax' (1979: 215). However, he uses the comparison solely as a descriptive device, and Janet Coleman justifiably notes that 'it explains nothing about imprinting and thought running over imprints' (1992: 53). As in the other works on artificial memory, the emphasis is on the technique of memorizing rather than on seeking to understand the nature of memory itself.

Although Quintilian praises artificial memory highly, he nevertheless remains sceptical of using such schemes in relation to memory for words. He argues that if a speech of some length is to be memorized, it is useful in the first instance 'to learn it piecemeal' (1979: 227), breaking it up into sections. Second, he recommends that an individual learn a passage by heart 'from the same tablets on which he has committed it to writing'. The mind's eye is then fixed not only on the words but on individual lines and also on places where the writing is 'interrupted by some erasure, addition or alteration': these marks act to 'prevent us from wandering from the track' (1979: 229, 331). Here, then, Quintilian is aware of the layout of writing as an aid to remembering and he seems to suggest embedding visual cues in difficult passages in order to stimulate the memory. As Carruthers points out, Quintilian 'effect[s] a transfer from the external tablet to the tablet of memory' (1990: 74). The script of external writing is thus intimately linked to the internal scripture of remembering. Unsurprisingly, Quintilian refers explicitly at this point in his argument to Plato's assertion that 'the use of written characters is a hindrance to memory'. He argues, on the contrary, for the efficacy of writing in the process of memorization: 'after writing for several days with a view to acquiring by heart what we have written, we find that our mental effort has of itself imprinted it on our memory' (1979: 217). There is, then, a marked difference between Quintilian's attitude to the artificial memory and that of Cicero and the author of *Ad Herennium* a century before. In relation to memory for words, Quintilian envisages not images located in an extensive place system but writing inscribed on a tablet or written on a page. Quintilian's interest in the visual presentation of the written word strikingly anticipates theories of memorizing in the medieval period, which I will discuss in the next section of this chapter.

I have so far outlined the 'art of memory' as it was elaborated in the key works of classical rhetoric. This tradition consciously builds on Aristotle's notion of recollection, to develop a system of memorizing that involves the methodical ordering of memory images and a search based on the principle of association. In the remainder of this section, I intend to focus on two key turning points affecting the subsequent fate of artificial memory. In both instances, mnemonics was brought into contact or union with Platonic reminiscence, which, as we have seen, is organized in relation to the higher realities or Ideas. I will turn first to St Augustine's *Confessions* (c. AD 398–400). In analysing this text, I will argue that the famous discussion of memory in Book X creatively and innovatively combines the rhetorical tradition of the place system and Platonic recollection. I will then trace the 'art of memory' to its furthest point in the so-called 'memory theatres' of the Renaissance. Frances Yates frames her celebrated account of Renaissance mnemonics, *The Art of Memory* (1966), with two examples of 'memory theatres': those of Giulio Camillo and Robert Fludd, both of which are indebted to the architectural spaces of the place system. As Yates points out, however, this late flowering of the 'art of memory' effectively transformed the trained and disciplined process of memorization into an 'alchemy of the imagination' (1966: 220). In what follows, then, I will trace the development of Platonic Idealism through Augustine's Christianizing of the Ideas and into the Renaissance Hermetic tradition.

St Augustine began his career as an orator and spent many years as a professor of rhetoric. It is therefore unsurprising that his account of memory is, in the words of Harald Weinrich, 'conceived entirely in the spirit of the ancient art of memory' (2004: 23). His discussion in the *Confessions* opens with the architectural imagery of memory as a 'spacious palace', a 'storehouse' in which the images derived from sense impressions are deposited and held (1961: 214). In his eloquent and expansive prose, Augustine describes himself as wandering through these 'vast cloisters', this 'immeasurable sanctuary' of memory (1961: 215, 216). His description thus evokes the buildings and spaces of the back-grounds used in the place system of remembering. Augustine is also preoccupied, as Yates points out, with the problem of images. He marvels that as he looks within he sees the whole universe reflected in his mind, so that not only are the seas, the stars, and the mountains present in his memory, but also 'the same vast spaces between them that would be there if I were looking at them in the world outside myself' (1961: 216). When he thinks of an object, such as a stone or the sun, these things are not present to his senses, but 'their images are present in my memory' (1961: 221). However, he puzzles whether 'health', memory', or 'for-getfulness', when they are named, are present in his memory as images or not. For Yates, Augustine's interest in whether notions are remembered with or without images is inseparable from 'the effort to find images for notions in the orator's mnemonic'. Likewise, she argues, the artificial memory is 'almost unconsciously implied' in Augustine's emphasis on the extraordinary capacity and invention of the mind (1966: 62). Other critics remain less convinced of Augustine's implicit reliance on the place system. For Carruthers, for example, the metaphors used by Augustine are 'archetypal' in nature and are not necessarily tied to the rhetorical tradition (1990: 146). However, there do seem to be clearly dis-cernible traces of the discourse of mnemonics in Augustine's account, even if he himself might prefer to banish the vain art of the orator from his more spiritual explorations.

In his investigation of the spaces of the mind, Augustine is not primarily concerned to elucidate the workings of memory, but rather to search for the presence of God. In questioning how God is present in the memory, Augustine's thought is suggestive of Plato. Moving on from memory derived from sensory experience, Augustine observes that memory also contains logical, gramma-tical truths. He does not know how these truths entered into his mind but, he argues, '[i]t was my own mind which recognized them and admitted that they were true'. Augustine's reflections recall Plato's *Meno*, but although he argues that these truths were already latent in his mind, he resists the idea that they existed there before birth. Rather, he claims, they were 'hidden away in its deeper recesses, in so remote a part of it that I might not have

been able to think of them at all, if some other person had not
brought them to the fore by teaching me about them' (1961: 218).
Augustine similarly describes the knowledge of God in terms that
evoke Platonic reminiscence. Again, however, Augustine resists
the notion that truth pre-exists in the mind from eternity. As
Janet Coleman explains, for Augustine the knowledge of God is a
truth 'learned at a particular moment, and since that time when
it was learned it has been stored in the memory' (1992: 90). In
the *Confessions*, Augustine's own moment of revelation comes when
he is conversing with his mother about the eternal life of the
saints. As they talk of the eternal Wisdom, he claims, 'for one
fleeting instant we reached out and touched it' (1961: 197). Here,
then, is the Platonic moment of communion with the Ideas, but
it takes place during Augustine's lifetime, rather than before his
birth. God was not in Augustine's memory before he learned of
Him; by implication, some men have never learned of God and so
cannot recall Him. In his account of memory, then, Augustine
brings the rhetorical tradition into contact with Plato, creating a
complex and intricate dialogue between the two. He borrows
elements from both memory discourses, but also revises or
rewrites each of them in the light of Christian theology.

The final phase of artificial memory was marked by the union
of mnemonics and hermetic secrets. The 'art of memory' was
effectively transformed into a magical or occult art. Renaissance
Neoplatonism was inaugurated in Florence in the late fifteenth
century by Marsilio Ficino and his followers. Ficino promoted
belief in the divinity of man's mind. Man, made in the image of
God, occupied in the Ficinian system a middle place between the
terrestrial and celestial realms. A system of correspondences
linked the stars and the lower world and man could traverse these
worlds, piercing with his mind the secrets of the divine. As these
ideas spread, the 'art of memory' was accordingly revised and
organized in relation to the higher realities. In line with Plato,
artificial memory was no longer confined to retrieving knowledge
that had been learned and stored away; rather it aimed at understanding celestial truths. As Paul Ricoeur intimates, however, the
price of this development lay in 'the transformation of reasoned
speculation into mystagogy' (2004: 65). Progressively freed from

its relation with and service to the past, the 'art of memory' had to all intents and purposes become an art of the imagination.

One of the most striking manifestations of the Renaissance 'art of memory' was the memory theatre of Giulio Camillo (c. 1532). This 'theatre', on display in Venice and later in France, comprised a wooden structure large enough to be entered by at least two people at once. Camillo's memory theatre still recognizably used the place system of classical mnemonics, in which images were placed onto backgrounds. For him, however, the backgrounds and images symbolized the whole celestial and terrestrial order. Camillo's theatre reversed the space of the Renaissance theatre building: the spectator occupied the place of the stage and looked out into the auditorium. This rose before him in seven levels, representing the seven measures of the world; each of these was in turn divided by seven gangways, symbolizing the seven planets. On each of these gangways were seven gates or doors and onto these numerous images were placed. The theatre thus offered a vision of the world. It allowed the mind, in the words of Frances Yates, 'to read off at one glance, through "inspecting the images", the whole contents of the universe' (1966: 159). It also acted as a mnemonic aid or device by which the nature and order of things could be imprinted on the mind, using places and images as in the classical manner.

Although Renaissance Neoplatonism quickly spread from Europe to England, it was not until the reign of James I that it was fully integrated into the memory system through Robert Fludd's two-volume *Utriusque Cosmi, Maioris scilicet et Minoris, metaphysica, physica, atque technica Historia* (1617, 1619). Fludd's work represents for Yates 'probably the last great monument of Renaissance memory' (1966: 311). Like Camillo, Fludd took the architectural form of the theatre as his starting point. He was also concerned to elaborate in his 'memory theatre' the correspondences that link the earthly and heavenly realms. Unlike Camillo, however, Fludd placed his spectator in the auditorium of the theatre, looking down on the stage. As Fludd outlined, his memory system was divided into two distinct but related spheres. The 'square art' corresponded closely to the classical 'art of memory', using buildings and placing images on them. The images were of corporeal things, and represented men, animals, or inanimate objects. When the images were of men or animals, Fludd, like the author of *Ad Herennium*, recommended that they be engaged in activity of some kind. In his discussion of buildings, Fludd opposed the use of fictitious or imaginary places, arguing that they confused memory and added to its task. Real buildings, then, should be used to form mnemonic backgrounds. The 'square art' combined in Fludd with the 'round art' which used magical or talismanic images of stars, of gods and goddesses associated with celestial influences, or of virtues and vices. The buildings of the 'square art' were placed on the spherical heavens and zodiac of the 'round art' and they were thereby organically related to the stars. In this system, then, the places and images were located in a divine order and appeared to be sovereignly and celestially chosen. Their supposedly pre-ordained order hid or concealed the arbitrariness of selection that is inherent in any system of inscription. As Ricoeur observes, the 'art of memory', carried to its furthest point, entailed a rejection of 'the weaknesses inherent in both the preservation of traces and their evocation' (2004: 66).

For Yates, one of the most important aspects of Fludd's memory theatre was his insistence on the use of real buildings. In Fludd's time, the great wooden public theatres which had housed the drama of the English Renaissance were still standing and in use. Yates accordingly speculates that Fludd's memory theatre 'contains, as a secret hidden within it' factual information about theatres such as The Globe, home of the Lord Chamberlain's Company of actors to which Shakespeare belonged (1966: 329). The places of Fludd's 'round art' represented the stars of the heavens and the images of the 'square art' were described as 'shadows', in which the objects and events of the lower world consisted. Yates observes the similarity to the Shakespearean stage which had a covering supported by columns, the underside of which was painted to represent the heavens. This theatre furnishing was known as the 'heavens', but was also sometimes referred to as the 'shadow'. Yates proposes that the Shakespearean stage itself can be read in the light of Fludd's mnemonic system, so that man plays his part on the 'square stage' of the terrestrial world overlooked by the 'round celestial world' of the heavens (1966: 351). Yates' analogy is suggestive, not least for our interpretation of the staging of Shakespearean drama, but she herself acknowledges that the comparison necessarily remains both tentative and speculative.

Certainly we can see strong analogies between the memory theatres of Camillo and Fludd. In both cases, the Renaissance theatre building is adapted to create a memory system. Camillo erects in the auditorium seven levels and seven gateways and decorates them with images, while Fludd invests the stage and its canopy with earthly and divine significance. Together, these two memory theatres represent the final flourish of the artificial memory system. By the Renaissance period, the 'art of memory' was seen to be laborious and unfashionable. Although Erasmus in his *De ratione studii* (1512) still conceded that the place system could aid the memory, he nevertheless asserted that the best memory was founded on study, order, and application. In particular, Erasmus was suspicious of the occult and magical practices of memory that had developed. Yates argues that, in the Renaissance, the 'art of memory' was 'dying out, killed by the printed book' (1966: 162). It is undeniably the case that profound changes in the organization of memory were brought about by the advent of print. However, Yates here risks propounding a version of Platonic dualism: the internal scripture of remembering is fatally undermined ('poisoned') by the external script of the book. In the final section of this chapter, I therefore propose to complicate this statement by outlining the ambiguous, symbiotic, and highly intricate relationship between memory and the book that was, as Mary Carruthers has persuasively argued, particularly characteristic of the medieval and early-modern periods.

MEMORY AND THE BOOK

In 'The Consequences of Literacy' (1968), Jack Goody and Ian Watt traced a series of distinctions between oral and literate societies. For them, oral societies are characterized by a cultural tradition which is transmitted through face-to-face communication. What continues to be of relevance to the society is held in memory, while the rest is usually forgotten. In what Goody and Watt refer to as a 'process of social digestion and elimination'

(1968: 31), historical information tends to be automatically adjusted to existing social relations, as it is communicated by word of mouth from one member of the society to another. Memories are transmuted even as they are transmitted, and evolve as the society changes. Although Goody and Watt recognize, and draw to the reader's attention, the existence of mnemonic devices in oral cultures that resist this overall process of transformation, including '[f]ormalized patterns of speech, recital under ritual conditions, the use of drums and other musical instruments, [and] the employment of professional remembrancers' (1968: 31), they nevertheless argue that non-literate cultures tend to be marked by an erasing or forgetting of that which is not of immediate, contemporary social relevance. Rather than a word-for-word, mechanical memorization, such societies function in terms of an inexact evocation or reconstruction of memory.

In contrast, literate cultures enforce a clearer, more objective distinction between the past and the present. The writing down of elements of the cultural tradition means that literate societies cannot discard or absorb the past in the same way. Faced with a permanent record of the past, members of these societies gain, in the words of Goody and Watt, a 'sense of the human past as an objective reality' (1968: 44). They also, notably, gain a sense of the inconsistencies and contradictions in the cultural tradition, which are no longer obscured by adjustments made by the oral reciter to accommodate his material to his audience. Significantly, Goody and Watt note that within a century or two of the Homeric poems being written down, many groups of writers appeared 'who took as their point of departure … that much of what Homer had apparently said was inconsistent and unsatisfactory in many respects' (1968: 45). This trend of thought suggested that these writers had determined to replace myth with something more consistent, which would reconcile apparent contradictions. For Goody and Watt, then, the rise of literacy entailed a discursive shift from myth to history, which began for the Greeks with Herodotus and was further developed by Thucydides. History provided a documented account of the past, which analysed inconsistencies and excluded unverified assumptions. Goody and Watt's contrast between myth, which is passed on through 'a series of interlocking face-to-face conversations' and which 'favour[s] consistency between past and present' (1968: 48), and history, which is inscribed and 'favours awareness of inconsistency' (1968: 49), seems indebted to Maurice Halbwachs' distinction between memory and history, to be discussed in Chapter 4. For Halbwachs, the memory of social groups is usually transmitted orally and emphasizes continuity, while history takes up its stance outside of oral traditions, even though it may draw upon them for evidence, and focuses on change and inconsistency. Goody and Watt also note that the proliferation of written records in literate societies means that what any one individual knows is a minimal part of what is available to the culture. In literate societies, therefore, the individual cannot participate fully in the cultural tradition. Their sense of a past which is too expansive to be absorbed or assimilated, but which cannot readily be discarded, draws in turn on Friedrich Nietzsche's vision of history, to be elaborated in Chapter 3, which regards history as a burden that we carry around with us and by which we are perpetually weighted down.

With the passage from oral to written transmission, memory therefore undergoes a profound transformation. Not only can literate societies no longer assimilate or transmute the past, but the past is set apart from the present making historical enquiry possible. However, Goody and Watt crucially note that in literate cultures writing does not simply supplant memory, but rather acts as a memorial aid or cue: '[t]here was ... a strong tendency for writing to be used as a help to memory rather than as an autonomous and independent mode of communication' (1968: 40). In particular, writing is linked for them to the emergence of mnemonic procedures related to word-for-word memorization. At the heart of this mental activity lies the list: a series of words, gestures, or concepts that are to be carried out in a certain order and that enable information to be stored in a manner that allows for easy retrieval. We have already seen that from antiquity the metaphor of memory as writing is remarkably persistent in the Western imagination. Under this governing model, writing was put at the service of memory and was itself conceived as a form or process of memorization.

In the medieval and early-modern periods, written and print culture developed rapidly alongside the oral as books became much more widely available than ever before. We might, then, expect to find that the book emerged in this period as an alternative to human memory, for it was increasingly possible to record in writing what had previously been memorized. This was not the case, however: in the medieval and early-modern mnemonic traditions, the book was intended as an aid to memory and its purpose was not to replace but rather to facilitate remembering. Mary Carruthers indicates that, somewhat surprisingly, the widespread availability of books in this period 'did not profoundly disturb the essential value of memory training' (1990: 8). On the contrary, it was expected that what was written in books should be committed to memory. Accordingly, the book was in part a mnemonic, designed to both provision and cue the memory of the reader. A concern to cultivate and train the memory thus passed directly from classical antiquity into medieval and early-modern culture and seemed, as Carruthers notes, remarkably 'independent of "orality" and "literacy"' (1990: 11).

Memory (*memoria*) referred in medieval culture to a trained and disciplined memory, educated according to a well-established pedagogical system. As in the classical authors, the material to be remembered was broken down into smaller elements that were short enough to be recalled. These were then arranged into a rigid and logical order, so that one could easily and quickly locate a piece of information that had been stored. Both the initial construction and internalizing of the memory scheme and the subsequent act of recollection were accompanied by a state of profound concentration. Departing from the classical system, however, the artificial memory was no longer associated with dialectics or rhetoric but with the realm of ethics. As Carruthers elaborates, training the memory was not simply a process of learning and storing information, although it was useful in this context particularly for preachers. Rather, it was in and through a trained memory 'that one built character, judgement, citizenship, and piety' (1990: 9). Accordingly, techniques of memorization were central to the medieval education. Children learned to write as a part of reading and memorizing, so that they were 'doing exercises on [a] wax tablet to complement the mental exercises performed on ... memory' (Carruthers 1990: 112). At university level, students studied from books open in front of them, but they were again engaged in the activity of memorizing the most important passages from them. To learn was to commit to memory, and various mnemonic methods were devised to help the student. Conforming to Goody and Watt's emphasis on the importance of the list in literate societies, glossaries, lexicons, and lists of various kinds proliferated in medieval culture.

Central to understanding the medieval artificial memory system is the recognition that it rested almost exclusively on the discussion of memory in *Ad Herennium*. Cicero's *De oratore* and Quintilian's *Institutio oratoria*, the other two main sources for the classical art, were not available to medieval scholars. As Frances Yates notes, this may be one important reason why medieval mnemonics was not as closely associated with rhetoric as the ancient sources (1966: 69). From *Ad Herennium*, which was wrongly attributed to Cicero, medieval scholars such as Thomas Aquinas and Albertus Magnus revived a version of the place system. As Carruthers makes clear, however, they understood the specific rules of this system 'in the light of a medievalized tradition' (1990: 122); specifically, the classical place system was reworked in relation to the physical constraints of the book. The classical mnemonic, which was tied to an architectural setting, was transformed by the medieval scholars into a flat surface or area divided into a grid system. Rather than walking mentally through a space, the rememberer had a frontal perspective onto a plane and took in the location at a single glance. In medieval mnemonics, then, the background of the place system took the form of a pictorial diagram or tabular layout in order to utilize the physical page as a memory aid. The page was divided into a grid-like arrangement of cells or boxes, rectangular in shape and set out in layers or tiers. The individual 'places' were divided from each other by a series of columns joined with arches, corresponding to the architectural imagery of *Ad Herennium*. Each was given a slight depth of field, in order to allow certain images to be closer or more dominant than others. Corresponding to the rules laid out in *Ad Herennium*, each of the places was distinguished by having a contrasting background and all were arranged in a rigidly schematic order. Each box was typically marked with a number or a letter of the alphabet, so that the individual could easily find his place and was able to move confidently around the grid.

These locations formed the background of the memory system onto which were placed the images of what was to be remembered. The images were arranged in groups of three, five, or seven, and comprised an active scene in which their relative positions acted to recall the order of the material with which they were associated. As in *Ad Herennium*, the images should be of extremes in order to be more memorable; hence, many of the images were of a surprisingly violent or sexual nature. As Carruthers points out, however, the use of obscene or frivolous images was not seen to be inappropriate to the moral and ethical purpose of memorization: 'titillation ... is a necessary component of the art of memory, serving pious functions such as meditation and preaching' (1990: 137). Medieval mnemonic thus revived the classical place system but used the framework of the page to provide a set of orderly places or locations. In medieval memory books, which were written by hand rather than printed like later Renaissance books, the frame or background remained constant, while the images changed from page to page. As in the classical 'art of memory', the same background was used and reused to memorize different sets of images. The written page was, in turn, designed to be internalized or written on the memory. Writing on the memory, by implication, should be as orderly and systematic (as easy to read) as what was written on the page.

Throughout classical and medieval accounts of artificial memory, retention and retrieval were stimulated most effectively by visual means. Memories were marked by pictorial devices and were stored away as images that could be 'seen' by the mind's eye. As I noted in the last section, Quintilian also spoke of the mnemonic utility of textual layout and design, proposing that one should mark important or difficult passages with signs or symbols. It seems that for Quintilian such marks were to be made externally as well as in the mind, for he recommended always using the same tablet to memorize a passage of text. Although Quintilian's work was not available to medieval scholars, his ideas correspond closely to memory advice in the Middle Ages. It is common in medieval manuscripts to find marginal marks, which pointed out to the reader a passage that he may wish to commit to memory. From the twelfth century on, such marks commonly took the form of the word 'nota', a mnemonic sign which signalled to the reader that he should mark the passage with his own associated image to help in memorization. Carruthers accordingly notes of the medieval book: 'the margins are where individual memories are most active, most invited to make their marks, whether physically ... or only in their imagination' (1990: 245).

Manuscript illumination is accordingly, for Carruthers, intimately related to the practice of making mnemonic images. The visual images surrounding the text encouraged the reader to make his own related mental images. They also served as a reminder of the memorial function itself. Particularly prevalent in decorated books were images of jewels, coins, birds, fruit, flowers (with insects gathering nectar), and scenes of hunting and fishing. Trained memory was the gathering of treasure into a storehouse; the reader hunted down and caged memories, like birds or animals; and, like a bee, the individual gathered nectar in order to furnish the cells of memory. As Carruthers notes, these images most often accompanied Bibles, psalters, or prayer books, books 'that especially need to be remembered' (1990: 247). The visual marginalia of medieval books were therefore inseparable from their mnemonic purpose, both symbolizing the value and importance of memorizing, and acting to stimulate the creation of mental images in the reader.

In medieval culture, then, the act of reading did not mean simply passing one's eyes over a page, but involved transferring its contents into memory so that the letters were inscribed within. Reading was a process of interiorization, which concerned making a work a part of oneself. The act of looking at the words on the page was described as *lectio*. It was also necessary, however, to engage in *meditatio*, which referred to the subsequent process of storage and retrieval. *Meditatio* was often described as an act of digestive rumination, so that texts were swallowed in portions small enough to be properly absorbed. Meditative reading involved gathering texts and storing them away as a series of short sequences. The ordering of texts resulted from the mnemonic scheme that was imposed on them by the individual reader. A single portion of text would be stored or referenced in association with a number of other textual fragments, so that passages committed to memory were located in several different settings and contexts. The gathering of memory fragments created a storehouse of examples, which impressed themselves upon the reader and helped to form his moral character. This was, in turn, articulated through expressive gestures and actions, which emerged out of and were defined by the remembered experience derived from books.

The literary work that developed out of and most powerfully reflected the medieval approach to memory was *The Divine Comedy* by Dante Alighieri (1265–1321). This text was from the outset explicitly concerned with problems of memory. In *The Divine Comedy*, Dante as narrator thus recounts his journey through the three realms of Hell, Purgatory, and Paradise. He encounters there the souls of the dead, who are in the precise place that has been allotted to them by divine justice. Dante converses with them and stores their stories in his memory, in order to recollect and repeat them in the cantos of his poem. Frances Yates has proposed that Dante's work emerged out of and imitated the place system of remembering. In *The Art of Memory*, she thus observes without further elaboration: 'Dante's *Inferno* could be regarded as a kind of memory system for memorizing Hell and its punishments, with striking images on orders of places' (1966: 104). Viewed in this light, Dante creates the souls of the dead that he meets on his journey as various memory images. In accordance with the rules for images, these figures are often striking in some way. The punishments of Hell, in particular, provide Dante with vivid sources of imagery that linger in the mind long after they have been read. These images are placed on the backgrounds of Hell, Purgatory, or Heaven and, as Dante follows his path, he retrieves them in the order in which they occurred. The rules for backgrounds make clear that they must be properly illuminated, so that the images are not too brightly or too dimly lit. However, as Dante descends into Hell, he finds that it is a dark realm, a 'blind world' (Dante 1970: 35), which threatens oblivion. He frequently cannot make out clearly the images that arise before him as he proceeds on his way. The heavenly sphere of Paradise also causes Dante difficulty, for here there is too much light. Dante is dazzled as he approaches the living light of God, and this again threatens his memory for the visual impressions lose their clarity and distinctness. As he finds himself in the presence of the Divine, Dante concludes that it is indeed beyond his ability to recall: 'my vision was greater than speech can show, which fails at such a sight, and at such excess memory fails' (Dante 1975: 375). Throughout *The Divine Comedy*, then, Dante both draws on and revises the memory places of the mnemonic tradition. The places visited provide, in the words of Ricoeur, 'so many way-stations for a meditating memory' (2004: 64). This memory was, in the first instance, the narrator's own, as he recollected and meditated on the journey that he had undertaken. In a broader sense, Dante's eloquent imagery of Hell, Purgatory, and Heaven also encouraged his reader to commit to memory the exemplary figures of virtue and vice with which they were presented, and to recollect the key tenets and teachings of the Christian tradition. The book was intended to be impressed upon the mind of the attentive and diligent reader, in order to provide a moral frame-work to guide his own path towards the divine.

The Divine Comedy clearly reflected the medieval practice of reading as an ethical act. By following Dante's journey, and by committing it to memory as the narrator himself has already done, the reader equips himself with a series of examples which can guide his own future behaviour and conduct. In her persuasive reading of Book V of the *Inferno*, Mary Carruthers argues that Dante also exemplifies the process of medieval reading in the indivi-dual encounters that he relates. At the core of the story of Paolo and Francesca is an act of reading, as Francesca tells Dante that she and Paolo read the story of Launcelot together 'for pastime' (Dante 1970: 55). Read properly, the tale of Launcelot and Guinevere should have offered an instructive example to the young lovers, re-creating an exemplary scene that they could then store in their memories. However, the pair did not read far enough in the text. They stopped at the moment when Guinevere kissed her lover, for at that point Paolo, overcome with desire, kissed Francesca. They therefore failed to learn that Guinevere's kiss had already been seen by the Lady of Malohaut, and that illicit love would inevitably be betrayed. Paolo and Francesca thus missed the key point of the passage; namely, that passion should be checked. Carruthers observes that Francesca presents their fault as that of 'one point' only (1990: 187). In medieval manuscripts, the 'point' was a mark of textual punctuation that divided off a passage to be memorized. The mistake of Paolo and Francesca lies not in misinterpreting the passage, but in failing to 'divide' it wisely for the purposes of meditation and recollection. Although Carruthers concedes that it seems excessive for the pair to be damned for what amounts to poor punctuation, the fault takes on a broader significance when viewed in the context of medieval mnemonics:

> [S]ince *divisio* [dividing] produced the building-blocks of memory, and hence of education and character, punctuation was not an altogether trifling affair. It was crucial ... to the intelligibility of a text, but it was also crucial ethically, given the role that memory played in the formation of moral judgements.
>
> (1990: 187–188)

The failure of Paolo and Francesca to read further, and thus to read properly, affects Dante so deeply that it causes him to lose consciousness when he hears the story: 'for pity I swooned, as if in death, and fell as a dead body falls' (Dante 1970: 57). The lovers' error thus takes on a (literally) overwhelming significance within the tradition of reading and memorizing that characterized the medieval culture out of which Dante's text emerged.

Mary Carruthers has observed that what struck her most forcefully in relation to medieval culture was that it did not make 'the slightest distinction in kind between writing on the memory and writing on some other surface' (1990: 30). With the possible exception of Plato's *Phaedrus*, the same is true in relation to all of the writers that I have discussed in this chapter. In memorizing, one writes on both inner and outer tablets interchangeably. Writing on the memory is viewed as necessary for one's reasoning ability and moral judgement; writing, in turn, helps memorizing, for the written words can act as memorial cues. Rather than acting as an external support or tool in relation to memory, writing thus acts as a form of memorization and is intimately and inextricably bound to it. Throughout *The Book of Memory*, Carruthers insists that medieval mnemonic systems *are* a form of writing. They make surprisingly literal the image of memory as inscription that originated as a condensed and playful metaphor in Plato's *Theaetetus*.

John Frow has found particularly valuable in Carruthers' work her refusal to make a qualitative distinction between oral and literate cultures. This, he argues, can act positively to counter theories that oppose 'memory' as an organic, ritualistic, timeless, and sacred realm, predominantly associated with oral culture, to 'history' as an abstract, plural, concrete discourse that is embedded in the written archive. As I will suggest in Chapter 4, when I look at the writing on collective memory of Pierre Nora, such theories tend towards a nostalgic essentialism, which too easily allies 'memory' with a lost and irrecoverable, predominantly oral culture. Frow also goes on, however, to propose two distinct figures through which we can imagine the relation between memory and writing. The first of these he terms a model of 'retrieval' (1997: 227). Based in the logic of the archive, this system operates in terms of deposit and storage. It supposes a direct relation between space and mental categories (memory traces are considered to be discrete objects stored in particular places in the mind) and it assumes the physical reality of memory traces. Frow elaborates three main problems with this conceptual model. First, he argues, it suffers from being too realist in its presumption that the past 'is accessible only because of its physical persistence as a trace'. Second, it supposes that 'meanings taken up are the repetition of meanings laid down', so that the past in this sense determines the present. Third, it is unable to account for forgetting other than as 'a fault or as decay or as a random failure of access' (1997: 227). It is, then, a conception of memory to which forgetting is merely incidental. This model of memory dominated in accounts of the 'art of memory' which developed in antiquity and, as we have seen, it continued to hold sway throughout the Middle Ages and into the Renaissance. For the writers studied in this chapter, memory is a system used for storage and retrieval, and the object to be located is precisely that which was initially laid down. Forgetting, in this system, results either from a fault in the storage system or from a decay in or misrecognition of the memory traces.

Frow opposes to this a second model which is based on 'textuality' (1997: 228). This is predicated on the non-existence of the past, which means that memory is no longer a recovery or repetition of physical traces, but a construction of the past under conditions determined by the present. Rather than retrieval, the logic in this system is that of 'reversibility': the linear, cause-and-effect, before-and-after time of the previous model is replaced by 'a continuous analeptic and proleptic shaping' (1997: 229). Meaning is constituted retroactively and repeatedly, and forgetting is embedded as an integral principle, for the activity of ceaseless interpretation involves both selection and rejection. Memory, in this instance, is no longer related to the past as a form of truth but as a form of desire. Together, these models correspond to the two main ways in which memory has been conceptualized in Western culture. The two systems intertwine, and continually surface and re-surface across different thinkers and historical contexts. In the context of this study, however, the 'textual' model proposed by Frow corresponds particularly closely with 'romantic memory' as it has recently been defined by Frances Ferguson. In the next chapter, I therefore intend to focus on the significant reconceptualization, which amounts almost to a reinvention, of memory in the work of the Enlightenment and Romantic writers.

2

MEMORY AND THE SELF

Following its final flourish in Renaissance Hermeticism, the traditional 'art of memory', which had functioned from the classical to the early-modern period, fell into disuse. Although the reasons for this were undoubtedly complex, Richard Terdiman notes that it was due, at least in part, to 'profound changes in social organization and hence in the information economy in Europe after the Renaissance' (1993: 16, n. 24). In discussing the decline of the 'art of memory', Terdiman opposes two contrasting models of memory which map closely onto John Frow's distinction, outlined at the close of the previous chapter, between the 'retrieval' model and the 'textual' model. For Terdiman, the 'art of memory' conforms to the model of memory as 'reproduction'; like Frow's notion of 'retrieval', this entails that memory, in its ideal form, simply reproduces exactly the content that was initially deposited or stored. As Terdiman points out, again echoing Frow, one problem with this model of memory is that it 'engages us in an infinite regress' (1993: 58); it is concerned above all with stasis and 'seeks to sustain content against the universal tendency of remembered material to drift entropically' (1993: 58, n. 42). Against this tendency towards the 'retention of the old', Terdiman argues that, with the waning of the classical mnemonic systems, memory passed beyond the 'reproduction' model and 'frankly declared itself as *representation*' (1993: 59; original emphasis). Like Frow's 'textual' memory, the 'representation' model recognizes that the very act of inscribing memory itself *'rewrites* the text that it makes available for rereading' (1993: 109; original emphasis). In inscribing, memory simultaneously transforms, so that a memory represents not a copy of an original but more precisely a version of it. In this chapter, my intention is to trace this emergent model of memory across selected authors of the period from the late seventeenth century to the early nineteenth century, namely John Locke, David Hume, Jean-Jacques Rousseau, and William Wordsworth. There is a new emphasis, in each of these writers, on how the past is (re)figured in memory; in their works, remembering does not simply reproduce an image of the past but necessarily adapts it in the process.

THE TURN INWARD

For a number of writers concerned with the transition from classical and early-modern mnemonic systems to the conception of memory at the emergence of the 'modern' period, John Locke occupies a pivotal position. Paul Ricoeur, for example, unequivocally argues that 'the equating of identity, self, and memory … is the invention of John Locke at the beginning of the eighteenth century' (2004: 97). This claim had earlier been posited by Frances Ferguson, when she stated that Locke identified 'the importance of memory for anchoring a sense of individual continuity over time' (1996: 509). As Ferguson goes on to outline, Locke's treatment of memory was novel because it meant that the persistence of memory, rather than a consistency of actions, behaviours, or appearances, marked the individual identity. An important consequence of this new sense of selfhood was that Locke 'freed individuals from having to repeat the same actions continually and introduced them instead to a vision of their own possible progress and development' (1996: 509). Here, then, we can clearly see the opening up of memory from the stasis favoured by the classical mnemonic system to a more temporal, narrative conception.

Ferguson underlines this implication of Locke's work by pointing out that memory 'provided a theater that one could regularly open to compete with the theater of immediate experience' (1996: 509). Memory is, crucially, concerned with holding up for comparison present and past experiences; far from simply reproducing an image of one's past, remembering represents a process of reflection upon it. Ferguson connects Locke's 'internalization of experience' and attention to memory as 'identical with reflection', to the 'phenomenal rise of literature' that followed and, in particular, to the emergence of the novel (1996: 510). The connections that she makes are clearly suggestive and wide-ranging. In the remainder of this chapter, my own investigations are necessarily more limited in scope. I nevertheless aim to trace the progress of what Ferguson has termed 'romantic memory' through the philosophical writings of Locke and Hume, considering how they in turn anticipate the treatment of memory in the canonical literary works of writers of the Romantic period.

Although the main focus of my discussion concerns Locke's influence on subsequent writers, it is nevertheless evident that his own writing on memory looks back to earlier conceptions. Most obviously, this takes the form of calling into question the classical mnemonic system. Thus in *Some Thoughts Concerning Education* (1693), Locke is firmly opposed to children 'getting things by heart to exercise and improve their memories'. He argues that this mechanistic practice is based more on 'old custom' than on 'good observation', and suggests that a good memory depends not on the habit of rote learning but on the child's constitution and natural strength of retention. Drawing on the familiar language of impressing and imprinting, Locke observes: 'An impression made on beeswax or lead will not last so long as on brass and steel' (Locke 1996: 133). If the surface on which the memory text is to be imprinted is unsuitable, Locke suggests that this faculty cannot be significantly improved by exercises of learning by rote; remembering can be facilitated only by interest ('what the mind is intent upon') and by method ('order') (1996: 134). Critical of memorizing for its own sake, which represents for him retrieval without reflection or understanding, Locke suggests that if this method is to be employed, it should be directed to a useful and virtuous end: 'it may do well, to give [children] something that is in itself worth the remembering and what you would never have out of mind whenever you call or they themselves search for it. This will oblige them often to turn their thoughts inward, than which you cannot wish them a better intellectual habit' (1996: 134–5). Here, then, Locke unequivocally contests both the value and the efficacy of the artificial memory system, particularly for the purpose of educating young children.

In *An Essay Concerning Human Understanding*, Locke turns to the spatial metaphors of the classical mnemonic tradition in order to (re)conceptualize memory. In the 'art of memory', as we saw in the last chapter, memory was conceived as a space, most commonly a building, through which the individual moved in the process of remembering, retrieving the objects that had been placed there. The classical tradition also commonly represented memory itself as a storage space or warehouse. In the fourth edition of the *Essay*, published in 1700, Locke initially describes memory as 'the storehouse of our ideas' and as 'a repository, to lay up those ideas, which at another time [the narrow mind of man] might have use of' (Locke 1997: 147). Locke here combines the spatial metaphor with an economic model of storage, also recognizable from antiquity. However, Locke immediately qualifies or complicates his spatial metaphor, observing:

> this *laying up* of our ideas in the repository of the memory, signifies no more but this, that the mind has a power, in many cases, to revive perceptions, which it has once had, with this additional perception annexed to them, that it has had them before. And in this sense it is, that our ideas are said to be in our memories, when indeed, they are actually nowhere, but only there is an ability in the mind, when it will, to revive them again; and as it were paint them anew on itself.
>
> (1997: 148; original emphasis)

In Locke's revised view, then, the memory becomes a repository for ideas that have ceased to be anything; a storehouse whose contents are stored nowhere until they are revived. It is only as they are present again before the mind that the ideas exist once more. Here, Locke engages with the problem that we first encountered in Aristotle of how we think about things in their absence, and he notably deploys the same metaphor of drawing or painting. However, as Michael Rossington points out, he also crucially reconfigures memory in this passage so that 'it is less a place than a function of the mind'; the capacity to recall at will past perceptions and to renew them again (2007a: 71). If Locke thus draws closely in his writing on classical and medieval mnemonics, it is often precisely to register his own discomfort with, and distance from, the figures that they most commonly deploy.

Most strikingly in the *Essay*, Locke contends the notion of innate ideas, which are derived from Platonic reminiscence. In a Christianized version of Plato's divine Ideas stamped onto the soul, the Scholastics argued that we are born with certain principles of religion or truth already imprinted in our minds. Locke devotes several hundred pages at the opening of the *Essay* to refute this notion. In a famous formulation, he asserts that the infant's mind is like 'white paper, void of all characters, without any ideas'. The only ideas that afterwards come into the mind derive from experience; for Locke, it is on this basis that 'all our knowledge is founded, and from that it ultimately derives itself' (1997: 109). Memory; then, cannot be innate, 'original characters, stamped on the mind' (1997: 92), but must be acquired, either by the imprinting on the mind of external things or by a subsequent process of reflection on them. Locke thus establishes the empirical project of the *Essay* precisely by refuting the doctrine of innate ideas, returning to and revising Plato's imagery of inscription and imprinting. As Joshua Foa Dienstag observes, Locke's refutation of the innate ideas also implicitly comprises a rejection of stasis. Divine ideas would necessarily have a timeless, unchanging quality; ideas which are not innate, on the contrary, can appear in and over time, suggesting development, narrative, plot. Dienstag accordingly argues that rebutting the doctrine of innate ideas at the beginning of the *Essay* 'enables [Locke] to give a diachronic, narrative element to his account of knowledge and self' (1997: 27).

Locke's account of memory, as it develops, seems to follow Aristotle more closely than Plato, sharing with him an empirical foundation and understanding. As in Aristotle, Locke's memories are explicitly of the past; they manifest themselves as ideas that have been 'formerly imprinted' and that have been 'taken notice of before by the understanding' (1997: 150). Even when memories have been long dormant, Locke asserts, this sense of their pastness is retained. Like Aristotle, Locke distinguishes between active recollection, the wilful search for a memory, and a more passive form of reminiscence. In recollection, the mind can revive past perceptions 'when it will' and here it seems that Locke has full confidence in the voluntarism of memory (1997: 148). However, as David Farrell Krell notes, active recollection is given 'short shrift' by Locke in the *Essay*, and his account quickly moves on to discuss a more passive form of remembrance in which memories emerge of their own accord (1990: 79). Often, Locke observes, this is the result of the affections or emotions, so that memories are 'roused and tumbled out of their dark cells' by 'some turbulent and tempestuous passion' (1997: 150). Here, then, we seem very far from the orderly and methodical associations of memory in Aristotle; the associative work of memory is non-intentional and seems to initiate a chaotic, if not threatening, chain of activity, which releases memories from the 'dark cells' within which they have hitherto been secured and confined.

Memory for Locke, as for Aristotle, has a physical basis and so can be adversely affected by illness. Initially, Locke closely echoes Aristotle in indicating the various causes that can affect the functioning of memory; he thus cites health ('the constitution of our bodies'), temperament ('the make of our animal spirits'), and mood or attentiveness ('the temper of the brain'). However, if such weaknesses are for Aristotle the exceptions to the rule, Locke emphasizes the natural tendency of impressions to fade, so that memory is inherently entropic: 'there seems to be a constant decay of all our ideas, even of those which are struck deepest, and in minds the most retentive'. Writing and inscription seem helpless in the face of this inexorable process of erasure; Locke figures our minds as 'tombs' where, even if the 'brass and marble remain', the 'inscriptions are effaced by time', and the imagery 'moulders away'. Even writing incised in marble, that most durable of materials, will shortly 'calcine ... to dust and confusion' (1997: 149). Locke makes clear that whole periods of an individual's history and past can be eradicated in this way, leaving scarcely a trace of themselves behind: 'ideas in the mind quickly fade, and often vanish quite out of the understanding, leaving no more footsteps, or remaining characters of themselves, than shadows do flying over fields of corn; and the mind is as void of them, as if they had never been there' (1997: 148). Here, then, the mind is like the 'white paper, void of characters' of the new-born infant; even past impressions can, through illness or a natural process of decay, simply vanish and be forgotten (Locke 1997: 109). In what follows, I aim to explore the consequences of such a process of oblivion for Locke's conceptualization of the self. As Frances Ferguson observed, the self is for Locke constructed around the continuity provided by memory. However, it seems that for Locke memory is neither as stable nor as continuous as this implies. Forgetting is both an integral part of, and a constant threat to, memory in his work; especially given that, without the co-operation of memory, all of the other faculties of the mind are, for him, in large part rendered useless.

Locke opens his discussion of identity in the *Essay* by defining the identity of a 'man'. He notes that it exists in 'a participation of the same continued life, by constantly fleeting particles of matter, in succession vitally united to the same organized body' (1997: 299). The identity of a 'man', then, conforms to a notion of substance and is dependent on bodily or physical continuity over time. However, Locke immediately distinguishes the concept of the 'same man' from that of the 'same person'; personal identity, the identity of the self, he argues, is a function of the continuity of consciousness:

> in this alone consists *personal identity*, *i.e.* the sameness of a rational being: and as far as this consciousness can be extended backwards to any past action or thought, so far reaches the identity of that *person*; it is the same *self* now it was then; and 'tis by the same *self* with this present one that now reflects on it, that that action was done.
>
> (Locke 1997: 302; original emphasis)

For Locke, then, personal identity is identical with remembering one's own actions. Identity is entirely synonymous with consciousness;

by extension, if the memory of a past event or experience cannot be recalled or summoned to mind, then it is not properly a part of the self: 'it is impossible to make personal identity to consist in anything but consciousness; or to reach any further than that does' (1997: 309).

Yet, as noted above, Locke does not overlook the fact of faulty memory, or even of the total loss of memory, in his account of identity. He recognized that we do not always have comprehensive memories, nor can we inevitably call to mind all that we have done. Thus, he observes that consciousness itself is susceptible of 'being interrupted always by forgetfulness', while even the best memories 'los[e] the sight of one part [of a memory] whilst they are viewing another' (1997: 302). In particular, Locke notes, our consciousness is interrupted by sleep, when we 'hav[e] no thoughts at all, or, at least, none with that consciousness which remarks our waking thoughts' (1997: 303). Dreams represent for Locke '[c]haracters drawn on dust, that the first breath of wind effaces' from our minds; once lost, they are 'gone forever, and leave no memory of themselves behind them' (1997: 116). In each of the instances that Locke cites, then, consciousness is crucially interrupted or disturbed, whether by forgetfulness, an inability to attend to all of a given memory at one time, or by sleep, and this leads him to question how such moments of oblivion can be accounted for in his understanding of the self.

Taking the most extreme case, that of a man who has entirely lost the memory of certain parts of his life, beyond any hope of retrieving them, Locke observes that while it was the 'same man' who did these actions, in as much as he has bodily continuity over time, yet it was not the 'same person', precisely because his consciousness does not extend to that period of his life. In this sense, for Locke, the amnesiac man cannot say of an event within the period affected by his condition, 'I did that'; for the 'I' could not properly be said to stand for the person or the self at that time. Locke resorts to a legal or forensic vocabulary in the *Essay* to underline his arguments, noting that the term 'person' represents, in this context, a man to whom we can ascribe responsibility for his past actions. For him, if a man cannot remember what he did, if his consciousness cannot extend backwards to cover the act, he cannot be held responsible for it: 'whatever past actions [the mind] cannot ... appropriate to that present *self* by consciousness, it can no more be concerned in, than if they had never been done' (1997: 312; original emphasis). He thus offers a conception of the self that is inextricably bound to consciousness, defined by its very ability to remember, and therefore to narrate, past experiences in the present. Crucially, however, within Locke's version of the self, as John W. Yolton observes, 'a man without a person – odd as this sounds – is possible' (1970: 156). In this notion, Locke encapsulates something of the profound disruptions of identity that can be encountered in cases of memory loss, for example severe amnesia or an advanced case of dementia. Here, the 'man' (or woman) may be clearly recognizable before us, even as the 'person', the individual whom we know and love, seems curiously and painfully absent.

Locke's connection between memory and identity has exerted a considerable influence on subsequent thinking in this area. Recent accounts have stressed, however, that there is a need for a more corporeal account of memory than Locke provides; in the words of Mary Warnock, 'memory ... inevitably brings in the physiological' (1987: 1). Mind and body are thus not separate, as Locke's exclusive focus on consciousness suggests; rather, the brain's functioning is necessarily both mental and physical at the same time. This desire to broaden Locke's focus is consolidated by recent research into the behaviour of amnesiac patients, which has found that while these individuals may no longer be able to consciously recollect past events, they nevertheless retain an unconscious, 'bodily' memory based on habit. Linda Grant describes the instance of a man with Alzheimer's disease who could not remember where he parked his car, nor could he recall the telephone number of his wife to call her and ask her to pick him up, or even the address of his house so that he could catch a bus or a taxi home. Nonetheless, he was able to find his way home by walking, for 'his topographical memory was unaffected', his body 'remembering' the route that he had so often walked before (1998: 136). Recent conceptualizations of memory may represent a broader, less exclusively conscious, phenomenon than in Locke's original conception, recognizing that the body also has its own capacity to retain and recall the past, but memory nevertheless remains a crucial underpinning for, and foundation of, our sense of self.

David Hume's account of memory in *A Treatise of Human Nature* (1739–40) consciously builds on and extends Locke, but also anticipates the work of the Romantic writers in closely allying the faculties of memory and the imagination. In the 'Introduction' to his *Treatise*, Hume declares his intention 'to explain the principles of human nature'; for him, this task necessarily precedes all other forms of enquiry since it serves to ground the remainder of our knowledge. The foundation for his exploration into human nature is one 'laid upon experience and observation' (2000: 4). There is, for him, no other source of knowledge besides experience and he will not accept as legitimate any claim to knowledge that extends beyond this. The elements of his philosophy are accordingly the immediate objects of thought, the 'perceptions'. He divides these in turn into 'impressions', which are forceful and lively, and 'ideas', which are the fainter images of impressions and causally dependent upon them. From this basis, Hume sets out to uncover in a systematic and methodical manner the secrets of the mind. At the outset of the *Treatise*, he readily admits that these secrets lie 'very deep and abstruse', and they will accordingly be arrived at only with the 'utmost pains' and exertions on his part (2000: 3).

In the *Treatise*, Hume initially seeks to distinguish between the properties of memory and the imagination. In 'Of the ideas of the memory and imagination', he notes that when an impression has been present within the mind, it returns there as an idea. If in its new appearance it retains a strong degree of its original vivacity, then it constitutes a memory; if, on the other hand, the original impression is faint and faded in the mind, then it conforms to the imagination. The ideas of the memory are thus more vivid for Hume than those of the imagination and seem clearly distinct from them: 'when we remember any past event, the idea of it flows in upon the mind in a forcible manner, whereas in the imagination the perception is faint and languid, and cannot without difficulty be perceiv'd by the mind steady and uniform for any considerable amount of time' (2000: 11). He further elaborates that the memory 'preserves the original form' of the initial impression, so that it has an aspect of veridicality; the imagination, in contrast, is not constrained by truth but is at '*liberty … to transpose and change its ideas*' (2000: 12; original emphasis).

Later in the *Treatise*, however, in a section entitled 'Of the impressions of the senses and memory', Hume revises his initial claims. Although he at first reasserts that 'the ideas of memory are more *strong* and *lively* than those of the fancy [imagination]' (2000: 60; original emphasis), he immediately qualifies this statement. Memory, when it returns to the mind after a long interval, is inevitably 'much decay'd, if not wholly obliterated'. No longer 'drawn in such lively colours', the memory seems 'very weak and feeble', and it is correspondingly difficult to determine whether the image concerned does indeed arise from the memory or whether it is rather a product of the imagination. In a contrary manner, the ideas of the imagination can acquire 'such a force and vivacity, as to pass for an idea of the memory'; Hume cites the example of liars who, by the frequent repetition of their imagined ideas, 'come at last to believe and remember them as realities' (2000: 60–1). The two faculties share an uneasy relationship and, in certain circumstances, they merge into and supplant one another. Hume concludes that we are, in the end, unable to definitively distinguish memory from the imagination. What we are left with is merely a '*belief*' (2000: 61; original emphasis), based on feeling a greater vivacity or immediacy of the ideas when they return to the mind, and it is this alone that identifies an idea as a memory rather than as a product of the imagination. The boundary between memory and the imagination therefore becomes profoundly unstable in Hume; memory, by implication, can no longer be relied upon to be faithful and historically accurate to the past that it records, and it therefore becomes difficult to 'know' the past, to distinguish clearly between remembered and imagined realities.

Hume turns to the question of memory and the self in the section of the *Treatise* entitled 'Of personal identity'. He begins by disputing the philosophical notion that we have continuous, direct impressions of ourselves. Such a claim implies that our idea of our own identity is nothing but a copy of an original self, an original which would necessarily be, Hume notes, 'constant and invariable' (2000: 164). Against this, Hume records what he perceives when he tries to encounter an impression of the self, observing that he cannot capture '*myself*' but only some particular perception. Extrapolating from his own experience, Hume observes in a famous and much-cited passage from the *Treatise*: 'I may venture to affirm of the rest of mankind that they are nothing but a bundle of different perceptions, which succeed each other with an inconceivable rapidity, and are in perpetual flux and movement' (2000: 164; original emphasis). We can never, then, encounter the self but only one of the fleeting and momentary perceptions that come into being and just as quickly pass away. The mind is for Hume analogous to a theatre with a constantly changing show; on its stage 'several perceptions successively make their appearance, pass, re-pass, glide away and mingle in an infinite variety of postures and situations'. Hume's image of the theatre, like Locke's invocation of the storehouse, is reminiscent of the buildings of the 'art of memory'. However, he similarly hastens to qualify his metaphor, pointing out that we can know the show ('the successive perceptions') only; we do not know either where in the mind this is located ('the place') or of what it consists ('the materials, of which it is compos'd'). Like Locke, even as he draws on the vocabulary of artificial memory, Hume simultaneously troubles or complicates the metaphor that he advances. He also notes that there are periods, as in sleep for example, when even these 'successive perceptions' are no longer there. If sleep represents for Locke an interruption of consciousness, it seems to signify for Hume a more radical cessation of his very existence: 'I [am] insensible of *myself*, and may truly be said not to exist' (2000: 165; original emphasis).

The 'self', insofar as it can be said to exist at all, consists for Hume of a succession of fleeting and momentary impressions, which at times cease altogether. He is therefore drawn to enquire why we are so strongly inclined to think of ourselves as a single, unified entity, 'to suppose ourselves possesst of one invariable and uninterrupted existence thro' the whole course of our lives' (2000: 165). Hume notes that it comes naturally to us to describe ourselves as one person; it is only after philosophical reflection and analysis that we come to realize that there is no 'real bond' unifying our perceptions (2000: 169). For Hume, then, personal identity consists in a process of association, of which we remain largely unaware until we reflect upon it, which fills out the gaps between our perceptions and thereby gives us the illusion of a durable and consistent existence: 'our notions of personal identity proceed entirely from the smooth and uninterrupted progress of the thought along a train of connected ideas' (2000: 169–70). These associations ('connected ideas') induce our cognition to jump from one perception to the other, and as a result of these transitions, the notion of the identity or 'self' arises. Faced with the fragmentation and potential dissolution of the self, its 'perpetual flux and movement' (2000: 165), memory and the imagination therefore conspire in Hume to reinforce the (necessary) illusion that there is a unity in our different perceptions over time, and thereby to overcome the essential discontinuity of human experience.

In this section, then, I have sought to elaborate the main contributions of Enlightenment philosophy to the conceptualization of memory. Through a reading of key works by Locke and Hume, I have demonstrated that memory becomes much more individualized in this period, and is intimately connected with a notion of the continuous self. Although memory is linked with a relationship to truth, this does not constitute the primary focus of the texts discussed and is, indeed, complicated by Hume's collapsing of the distinction between memory and the imagination. Rather, memory's significance is located in its assertion of the singular identity of the individual across different times and places, and in the face of continual lapses and confusions. This emphasis is consistent across Locke and Hume; even if it constitutes for Hume an illusion or fiction, it is nevertheless one that is perceived to be necessary to our ability to function in the world. It is in the context of the new importance accorded to the unified being, fictive or otherwise, that the deficiencies of memory take on a particular charge in the work of the Enlightenment philosophers: the problem of sleep as a lapse in consciousness troubles the account of the self in both Locke and Hume, and it is accordingly a phenomenon to which they repeatedly return. Memory is valued in the Enlightenment, then, not for the ability to recall knowledge that has previously been stored, nor even for the capacity to affirm that past events have taken place, but rather for the possibility of reflexiveness itself; the ability, as Frances Ferguson has described it, 'to produce facts with personal application, ... the ability to move from one description to another' (1996: 514). It is, in turn, intimately bound to narrative; to remember is to be able to relate one incident or episode to another, and thereby to produce a version of the self. For Hume, however, this also entails that what we term the 'self' is inherently a narrative or fiction, composed of a multiplicity of individual descriptions which are linked or threaded together along complex chains of association. In the following section, I move on from the thinkers of the Enlightenment to address the convergence of memory, narrative, and individual identity in the writing of Jean-Jacques Rousseau. I argue that, in his *Confessions*, he constructs a version of the self precisely from a seemingly exhaustive elaboration of individual events or incidents. At the same time, however, he is intensely aware of, and intimately concerned with, identifying the threads or chains of association which connect these incidents together, and by and through which his own behaviours and habits, indeed his very personality itself, have been uniquely formed.

ROUSSEAU'S CHAINS OF ASSOCIATION

In her study of eighteenth-century autobiographical discourse, Felicity Nussbaum has observed that the conception of 'self' was both complex and contested in this period. She thus remarks: 'In eighteenth-century England, "identity", "self", "soul", and "person" were dangerous and disputed formations, subject to appropriation by various interests' (1989: 38). In the preceding section, I demonstrated that Enlightenment philosophy, in addition, presented a fundamentally contradictory and divided view of identity: for Locke the self existed through and over time, while for Hume its very existence was uncertain and open to question. The emergence of autobiographical writing provided an intensely self-reflexive mode of discourse through which these tensions and uncertainties surrounding the self could be displayed and mediated. For Nussbaum, autobiographies represented not a 'benign search for an essential "self"' but rather a 'private occasion and later a public forum for attempting to resolve ... problems [of identity]' (1989: 38). For Laura Marcus, likewise, eighteenth-century auto-biographies 'both consolidate[d] and question[ed] emergent/dominant definitions of identity' (1994: 16). In this section, I intend to focus on Jean-Jacques Rousseau's *Confessions* (1782–89), a central, if not founding, text in the genre of Romantic autobiography. Rousseau here presents a succession of related incidents, which together make visible the development of his individual life-history. However, his account of his passage through time is simultaneously portrayed as a process of constant adjustment and mutation, so that the 'self' is to some degree undone even as it is advanced. I argue that, simultaneous to the development of a modern 'individualism', Rousseau's autobiography provides a way of ordering and objectifying the 'self', but that it also necessarily reflects its inherent conflicts and vacillations.

In his *Confessions*, completed in 1770 and published post-humously between 1782 and 1789, Rousseau famously sought to reveal himself entirely and with complete transparency to his readers. In the celebrated opening passage of his autobiography, he thus observed:

> I have resolved on an enterprise which has no precedent, and which, once complete, will have no imitator. My purpose is to display to my kind a portrait in every way true to nature, and the man I shall portray will be myself.
>
> Simply I know myself. I know my own heart and understand my fellow man. But I am made unlike any one I have ever met; I will even venture to say that I am like no one in the whole world. I may be no better, but at least I am different.
>
> (Rousseau 1953: 17)

In order to accomplish his stated aim, to 'display' himself fully to his readers, it was necessary that nothing in his life should remain obscure or hidden from view. Rousseau accordingly aimed in his narrative towards comprehensiveness: his account of himself accumulated details and paid attention to even the most seemingly trivial incidents. As Ann Hartle observes, it was imperative that there should be 'no voids, no gaps, no occasion for asking "What was he doing during that time?"' (1983: 94). Such a narrative conception seems logically to be founded upon the premise that memory can effortlessly call to mind everything that has happened, that nothing has been forgotten or lost, that there have been no lapses in consciousness. It is notable, then, that although his narrative appears entirely coherent, Rousseau openly acknowledges that there are breaks in his memory. At the end of Book III, he thus remarks that even though some events remain as vivid to him 'as if they had just occurred', there are nevertheless many 'gaps and blanks' in his memory, which, he admits, 'I cannot fill'. He does not regard this as a problem, however, for he crucially goes on to observe: 'But over everything that is really relevant to the subject I am certain of being exact and faithful' (1953: 128). Gaps in memory do not trouble him, it seems, because anything that has slipped from his memory is by definition unimportant and inessential. As Jean Starobinski remarks, it is not until we reach Freud and Proust that slips or lapses of memory take on their own significance; that, in his words, 'a forgotten event hides an essential truth' (1988: 181).

For Rousseau, memory can give him access to events in his life, events which no longer exist but which can be vividly recalled. In his mature years, this faculty provides him with much-needed consolation: in calling to mind recollections of better times, he is able to relive something of their former intensity. At the opening of Book VI, for example, Rousseau observes that his stay in the household of Madame de Warens was so happy that 'nothing I did, said, or thought all the while it lasted has slipped from my memory'. He is accordingly able to recall this period 'in its entirety, as if it existed still' (1953: 215–16). To exemplify his 'vivid and precise' memories relating to this phase of his life, Rousseau recounts that some twenty-five years later, on encountering a periwinkle while out walking, he was immediately returned in his mind to an earlier walk with Madame de Warens, when she had originally pointed out the flower to him. The modest blue periwinkle thus acts in a way that prefigures Proust's madeleine, to resurrect an earlier environment with remarkable 'strength and precision' (1953: 216); although Starobinski notes that Rousseau does not, like Proust, make 'the effort of understanding necessary to grasp the essence of time' (1988: 236). Memory, then, is valued by Rousseau for the access that it provides to his past, which can be vividly recalled and relived. However, the imagination is accorded an equal importance in his work, for it alone gives him access to his interior self. Introducing the second part of the *Confessions*, Rousseau contends that his true object is not merely to 'transpose facts' but to 'reveal my inner thoughts'. Memory is of secondary importance to this aspect of his project: '[i]t is the history of my soul that I have promised to recount, and to write it faithfully *I have need of no other memories*; it is enough if I enter again into my inner self, as I have done till now' (1953: 262; emphasis added). Here, then, it seems that Rousseau wishes to communicate a truth that is concerned not with the veracity of remembered biographical detail, but with the past as it exists within him in the form of present feeling and emotion.

Jean Starobinski's influential study *Jean-Jacques Rousseau: Transparency and Obstruction* (1988) focuses on this and similar passages from the *Confessions* to argue that Rousseau's primary purpose in his autobiography is to reveal his own inner truth. However, Rousseau's project is inevitably compromised for Starobinski by the contradictions and paradoxes that are inherent in language itself. These necessitate that, in order to communicate himself as he is, Rousseau must, in his own words, 'display myself as I was' (1953: 17); he is forced to reveal the present self suspended along the extended chain of narrative time:

> He displays, spread out over biographical time, the truth that feeling takes in at a glance. The unity and simplicity of that truth are unravelled in a multitude of instants lived one after the other in order to show how a single life governs and therefore gives unity to his character. He must show how he came to be the person he is.
>
> (Starobinski 1988: 188)

For Starobinski, then, Rousseau's autobiography, in resorting to the serial presentation of what is essentially instantaneous, reveals a reluctant complicity with the dictates imposed by language. His reading relegates the narrative element of the *Confessions* to the

status of a necessary evil, adopted by Rousseau for purely contingent and pragmatic reasons. Michael Sheringham rightly comments, however, that Starobinski's exclusive emphasis on a single
aspect of Rousseau's 'notoriously multi-faceted' thought under-
values alternative strands and possibilities. Sheringham specifically draws attention to Rousseau's endeavour 'to give expression
to a historicized self, a selfhood inseparable from the twists and
turns of its story' (1993: 33). In the remainder of this section, I
accordingly seek to offer an alternative reading of Rousseau, which
follows Sheringham in focusing precisely on the narrative 'twists
and turns' of his autobiography. I pay particular attention to the
story that Rousseau tells of his childhood years, for it is here that
we can most clearly perceive the patterns of linkage and development in past experience through which the self is constructed,
but here also that disruptions and discontinuities are revealed, so
that the self is simultaneously unravelled and undone.

If Rousseau reveals the self in and through narrative, the specific form that he adopts for his autobiography is that of the
'confession'. His title deliberately refers back to Augustine, and
Huntington Williams accordingly notes that Christian autobiography forms an 'implicit background' for Rousseau's writing
(1983: 2). At the opening of his text Rousseau appropriately
postures before God, autobiography in hand, invoking the image
of the Last Judgement as a guarantee of his veracity:

> Let the last trump sound when it will, I shall come forward with this work
> in my hand, to present myself before my Sovereign Judge, and pro-
> claim aloud: 'Here is what I have done, and if by chance I have used
> some immaterial embellishment it has been only to fill a void due to
> a defect of memory. I may have taken for fact what was no more than
> probability, but I have never put down as true what I knew to be false.
> I have displayed myself as I was, as vile and despicable when my
> behaviour was such, as good, generous, and noble when I was so. I
> have bared my secret soul as Thou thyself hast seen it, Eternal Being!'
> (Rousseau 1953: 17)

It quickly becomes apparent, however, that Rousseau's intended
interlocutor here is his reader; it is, after all, the reader who will

weigh the facts of his case, 'assemble [its] elements and ... assess the being who is made up of them' (1953: 169). Rousseau's address to the Almighty seeks to impress upon his reader the weight and gravity of his task, and Williams accordingly notes that Rousseau 'follows the tradition of confessional literature only in form' (1983: 187).

Rousseau's departure from Christian autobiography is particularly evident, as Ann Hartle has persuasively argued, in his treatment of narrative causation. Augustine's belief in providence is central to his *Confessions*, which are founded on the conviction that God has ordered the course of his life, leading him to where he is now. Augustine is certain that there is a divine purpose or design in his life, even if he himself cannot perceive it in its entirety, and he therefore seeks to recount selected incidents from his life in and through which, he feels, God's providence makes itself manifest to him. For Rousseau, by contrast, the order of the events in one's life cannot be traced back to God's providential intentions. The alternative that he advances becomes evident, as Sheringham has noted, in his description of two closely related incidents from his early childhood: his spanking by Mademoiselle Lambercier for an unnamed childish misdemeanour, and the subsequent beating by her father when he had been accused, falsely he claims, of breaking a comb. Rousseau famously argues that his beating by Mademoiselle Lambercier formed his sexual inclinations; in this incident, corporal punishment and sexual pleasure come together and remain bound to one another, influencing the whole of Rousseau's subsequent emotional life:

> Who could have supposed that this childish punishment, received at the age of eight at the hands of a woman of thirty, would determine my tastes and desires, my passions, my very self for the rest of my life, and that in a sense diametrically opposed to the one in which they should normally have developed?
>
> (Rousseau 1953: 26)

However, the subsequent beating by Mademoiselle Lambercier's father, although seemingly similar, produces entirely the opposite effect, for Rousseau attributes to this incident the origins of his lifelong abhorrence of injustice: 'the memory of the first injustice I suffered was so painful, so persistent ... that, however strong my initial bent in that direction, this youthful experience must certainly have powerfully reinforced it' (1953: 30). Rousseau thus makes clear that two similar incidents, occurring at the same period in his life, produce radically different effects because of the varying circumstances surrounding them. He summarizes the case as follows:

> When I trace my nature back in this way to its earliest manifestations, I find features which may appear incompatible, but which have nevertheless combined to form a strong, simple, and uniform whole. I find other features, however, which, though similar in appearance, have formed by a concatenation of circumstances combinations so different that one could never suppose them to be in any way related to one another. Who could imagine, for instance, that I owe one of the most vigorous elements in my character to the same origins as the weakness and sensuality that flows in my veins?
>
> (Rousseau 1953: 28)

For Rousseau, then, the fixed and unvarying narrative of providence gives way to a complex, shifting model of causation, in which events, feelings, and circumstances combine and modify one another in unexpected and seemingly haphazard ways. Rousseau's *Confessions* thus return to and rewrite Augustine's notion of a single divine purpose, seeking to demonstrate instead the multiple, and at times contradictory, pathways of causation that converge at any given phase of his existence.

Rousseau's account of his early childhood punishments in the household of Mademoiselle Lambercier prefigure and prepare the ground for what is arguably the most celebrated episode in the *Confessions*: the incident of the stolen ribbon. In Book II, Rousseau recounts that, when he served as a valet in the household of Madame de Vercellis in Turin, he stole a little pink and silver ribbon. When the ribbon was subsequently found among his possessions and he was accused of the crime, Rousseau blamed the theft on a maidservant named Marion, with the result that they were both dismissed from their respective positions. Rousseau claims in his defence that he was left out of the will of Madame de Vercellis; that he named Marion because 'she was the first person who occurred to me'; that he, in fact, intended to give the ribbon to Marion; that he was thrown into '[u]tter confusion' by being publicly confronted with the crime; that his accusers sought to deliberately 'frighten' him, and that he was 'scarcely more than a child' at the time that the incident occurred (1953: 88–9). A number of critics have remarked, however, that Rousseau's account of his false accusation multiplies its possible causes to such a degree that the episode resists assimilation into the broader narrative. Michael Sheringham accordingly terms it a 'wild incident' in the autobiography, which acts to 'jeopardize conventional, linear, narrative order' (1993: 104), while for Huntington Williams it represents a 'bad stor[y]' which 'can never be redeemed' (1983: 138). It certainly seems that Rousseau, in accumulating such a multitude of excuses, wishes to convince us that he would have acted differently if only the circumstances had been different; indeed, he goes as far as imagining alternative scenarios in which he was 'allowed time to come to my senses', and in which other, kinder words were spoken to him by his accusers (1953: 88–9).

Of all the recounted incidents in the *Confessions*, Rousseau singles out the theft of the ribbon as of particular personal and affective significance. He claims that he has never before revealed it to anyone, and argues that 'the desire to rid myself of it has greatly contributed to my resolution of writing these *Confessions*' (1953: 88). Here, then, Rousseau assumes that the act of confession has the power to 'rid' him of his past: his crime is recalled precisely in order that it might be obliterated through absolution. '[C]onfession', as Richard Terdiman observes, 'is an act of memory that seeks to neutralize memory; in confession one remembers *in order to forget*'. However, Terdiman notably goes on to argue that the *literary* confession works to subvert the expectations of the ritual act of confession on which it draws. Here, the past is specifically recalled for public circulation and consumption, and the inscribing of the fault means that it cannot easily be forgotten or erased. In the confessional autobiography, Terdiman notes, the 'impermanence' of the confessional act is 'transformed, indeed overturned' (1993: 77; original emphasis). Paul de Man argues similarly, in his reading of the *Confessions*, that Rousseau's literary revelation of his childhood theft is 'not primarily ... confessional' (1979: 279). Rousseau tells us of his crime in the confessional mode, but this does not suffice for him; he is also drawn, at the same time, 'to put up such excuses for myself as I honestly could' (1953: 88). Although in Rousseau's 'confession' of the theft there is evidence of a crime (the ribbon was stolen), his excuses relate to his inner feelings both past and present; in the absence of any evidence or proof of these, we simply have to trust in what he chooses to tell us. De Man thus distinguishes in Rousseau between a cognitive mode of confession, which operates referentially, and a rhetorical or performative mode of excuse, which produces verbal utterances that cannot be verified. Where the confession seeks to close off the past, so that Rousseau's stated aim is to 'rid' himself of his crime, the excuse fails to satisfy or to contain meaning, with the result that memory is always open to further expansion and repetition. The rhetorical, performative aspect of Rousseau's text means that he cannot effectively neutralize the memory that he recounts; although his stated aim is to leave the subject of the theft safely behind, so that he closes Book II with the hope that he '[m]ay ... never have to speak of it again' (1953: 89), he nonetheless tells the entire story over again some ten years later in the fourth Promenade of the *Reveries*.

If Rousseau identifies any one discernible feeling in relation to the incident of the ribbon, it is, de Man notes, '*shame* about himself rather than any hostility towards his victim' (1979: 283; original emphasis). According to his own 'confession', Rousseau had blamed Marion because of his desire for her: the ribbon was intended to be given to her as a gift. De Man therefore questions what is so shameful in revealing this desire; if Rousseau's account is true, he argues, then 'the motivation for the theft becomes understandable and easy to forgive' (1979: 284). Yet Rousseau moves on to suggest in the latter part of his story that both Marion and the ribbon are, in actuality, insignificant to him; his desire is located elsewhere, and de Man accordingly asserts that '[w]hat Rousseau *really* wanted is ... the public scene of exposure which he actually gets' (1979: 285; original emphasis). His shame acts as an excuse for Rousseau to 'expose' himself in writing; this desire is truly shameful, because it means that Marion was destroyed 'merely in order to provide him with a stage on which to parade his disgrace or, what amounts to the same thing, to furnish him with a good ending to Book II of his *Confessions*'. For de Man, then, Rousseau's text itself generates guilt in order to justify the excuse, in a process which is endlessly self-perpetuating, 'for each new stage in the unveiling suggests a deeper shame, a greater impossibility to reveal, a greater satisfaction in outwitting this impossibility' (1979: 286). Following de Man's logic to its conclusion, the actual content of Rousseau's confessions ceases to matter, so long as the text continues to provide him with a stage on which he is able to play out his inner drama.

De Man's reading of Rousseau demonstrates that excuses paradoxically generate the very guilt that they claim to exonerate; thus, instead of expiating his crime, Rousseau's multiple excuses lead him into further anxiety when he speculates on the possible fate of Marion following her dismissal: 'the memory tortures me less on account of the crime itself than because of its possible evil consequences' (1953: 89). Although he does not know what has happened to Marion, he is convinced that it can be nothing good and he accordingly speculates on her life in increasingly gloomy terms:

> [S]he cannot possibly have found it easy to get a good situation after that. The imputation against her honour was cruel in every respect. The theft was only a trifle, but after all, it was a theft and, what is worse, had been committed in order to lead a boy astray. Theft, lying, and obstinacy – what hope was there for a girl in whom so many vices were combined? I do not even consider misery and friendlessness the worst dangers to which she was exposed. Who can tell to what extremes the depressed feeling of injured innocence might have carried her at her age?
>
> (Rousseau 1953: 87–8)

What is notable in this description is that Rousseau's memory extends beyond the capacity to retrieve or record events. Rather, it involves a moral obligation on his part to re-examine his past action in order to see whether its meaning or value has been changed by what has, or may have, subsequently taken place. He reviews his former action, his false accusation of Marion, in relation to a variety of different, although similarly woeful, sets of consequences; his memory is thus concerned not so much with what he was conscious of at the time that he made the accusation, but with all that he can either know or imagine about its aftermath. This form of remembering is intimately allied to Ferguson's definition of 'romantic memory', which represents, she argues, 'the power of seeing a past that one didn't experience at the time of its occurrence' (1996: 533). Rousseau's description of the stolen ribbon looks back on a past which appears very different from his present perspective; the incident is captured so vividly precisely because it is viewed in retrospect, in the light of what has, or could have, happened since. Although many of the effects that Rousseau supposes his action to have had were unmeant at the time, and even though he does not know whether or not his worst imaginings relating to Marion are true, he nonetheless suffers, or is tortured, *as if* the possible consequences had been fully intended. As he himself observes: 'I took away with me lasting memories of a crime and the unbearable weight of a remorse which, even after forty years, still burdens my conscience' (1953: 86).

Ferguson argues that the disadvantage of such an expansive form of memory, which takes in the past action and all of its possible consequences, is that it has no limit; it could potentially 'expand forever' and so produce 'a kind of anticipatory guilt of massive – indeed, paralyzing – proportions' (1996: 529). As a consequence of this, she contends that romanticism brings an increasing pressure to bear on memory to 'provide convincing evidence *that one hasn't acted*, that one hasn't yet seen things that would make one regret one's past for the consequences that have attended it' (1996: 528; original emphasis). An alternative form of remembering, which is termed by Ferguson 'circumstantial memory', thus acts as a balm or corrective to a memory which produces more guilt than it can contain, by clustering evidence around the description of an event in order to resist its assimilation to narrative. 'Circumstantial memory' seeks to demonstrate, in Ferguson's words, precisely 'that *there is no news*, that nothing has happened' (1996: 529; original emphasis). In this context,

Rousseau's anxious concern to list all of the possible circumstances surrounding his accusation of Marion can be interpreted as a means of disrupting the narrative, resisting its capacity to produce events. Likewise, as he speculates on Marion's fate, concluding her story with a suggestion of the worst extremes to which she may have been driven, the bewildering variety of proffered outcomes acts to hold the narrative open, prevents us from settling on any one consequence, implies that we do not and cannot know what has happened; and, indeed, perhaps nothing has. Although Ferguson does not specifically refer to or discuss Rousseau in this context, the *Confessions* can thus be seen to closely correspond to, if not inaugurate, the paradoxes and contradictions of 'romantic memory', as she has defined and described them.

Rousseau is central to the concerns of this chapter because his *Confessions* represent the origins of modern, Romantic autobiography; as Huntington Williams notes, Rousseau 'occupies a pivotal position historically ... because he attempts to construct his personal identity primarily in his own writings' (1983: 3). Although Augustine, to whom Rousseau looks back in the title of his work, seems to have initiated a literature of the self, I argued in the previous chapter that his conception of inwardness draws on the architectural spaces, the rooms and buildings, of the classical mnemonic tradition. Ricoeur thus remarks that '[i]t is not yet consciousness and the self, nor even the subject, that Augustine describes' (2004: 98); we see these articulated first in Locke, and they subsequently find a more literary form and expression in Rousseau. Building on the foundations of Enlightenment philosophy, Rousseau's memory connects a self dispersed across markedly different times, places, and circumstances. He is concerned, however, not merely with recounting successive events but with revealing an inner truth. His *Confessions* are, he states, the story of his feelings; and, in this, he reacts against Enlightenment empiricism, which is based in an exclusively objective experience of the world. Rousseau is intimately tied to the tradition of 'romantic memory', for he continually asserts the uniqueness and singularity of the individual. It is notable, however, that the memory that most profoundly haunts and troubles him, the incident of the stolen ribbon, primarily concerns the effects of his actions on another person. Here, then, individualism is complicated and disrupted by the necessary entanglement of the self with others. For Ferguson, this too typifies 'romantic memory', which invariably 'includes reference to the claims of the collective' (1996: 510). The existence of other people, she contends, 'continually enables one to assume a constantly escalating set of moral liabilities that constitutes an oppressive burden on the individual' (1996: 530). I have argued above that this surprisingly 'oppressive' form of memory, in which the individual is always already bound to others, can be clearly identified in Rousseau's *Confessions*. For Ferguson, however, this memory 'finds some of its starkest and most exact illustrations ... in Wordsworth's poetry' (1996: 525). It is, accordingly, to Wordsworth's writing on memory, and specifically to the poem 'Tintern Abbey', that I turn in the next and final section of this chapter.

'THE PICTURE OF THE MIND REVIVES AGAIN'

'Lines written a few miles above Tintern Abbey, on revisiting the banks of the Wye during a tour, July 13, 1798' is a poem centrally concerned with memory. Wordsworth is interested in the process of memory as the signification of something absent by its mental image, and he accordingly highlights throughout the poem a complex interplay of presence and absence. The speaker begins with an apparently straightforward description of the present scene that he surveys. Even here, though, as David Bromwich has noted, the insistently repeated word 'again' alerts us that this is a landscape revisited; it is a repetition of an earlier scene, in which the speaker finds both comfort and solace (1998: 86). It soon becomes clear, however, that the restorative power of the pastoral scene derives not from its immediate impression upon the senses, but rather from memory images stored in the mind. It is only when the speaker has been long 'absent' from the scene (l. 23) that the images can become a vehicle of both emotion and understanding:

> But oft, in lonely rooms, and mid the din
> Of towns and cities, I have owed to them,
> In hours of weariness, sensations sweet,

Felt in the blood, and felt along the heart,
And passing even into my purer mind
With tranquil restoration.

(ll. 26–31)

Memory, then, seems to operate most effectively at a spatial and temporal distance from its past object. Likewise, although memory involves continuity with the past, so that the speaker is able to connect his earlier visit with the present one and thereby create a sense of having a history, the poem also registers an intense awareness of the transformations that have occurred between the two encounters. Memory is concerned with holding up past and present experiences for comparison; it enables the speaker to chart an ongoing process of alteration, both in the landscape before him and within himself. In this sense, then, 'Tintern Abbey' does indeed provide, in Ferguson's terms, an 'exact illustration' of the workings of 'romantic memory' (1996: 525), for it enables the speaker to reflect upon past experience from his present perspective and to register that he himself is 'changed … from what I was, when first / I came among these hills' (ll. 67–8).

It is notable, however, that as the poem enters its final section – the address to Dorothy, who shares the present experience with him – Wordsworth comes to see himself as, in Tilottama Rajan's terms, having 'close[d] the fissure created by time within the self' (1980: 219). His turn towards Dorothy, his younger sister, is instrumental to the transition at the end of the poem, for in embodying or incarnating the past, she represents a redemptive continuity between past and present:

For thou art with me, here, upon the banks
Of this fair river; thou, my dearest Friend,
My dear, dear Friend, and in thy voice I catch
The language of my former heart, and read
My former pleasures in the shooting lights
Of thy wild eyes. Oh! Yet a little while
May I behold in thee what I was once,
My dear, dear Sister!

(ll. 115–22)

For Rajan, the closing address to Dorothy locates 'Tintern Abbey' within the genre of the 'conversation poem'. Typical of this genre, she contends, are poems which begin by asserting the alienation of the speaker, through physical or temporal separation, from a scene of nature that is envisaged as past or future rather than present. The poems usually end with a benedictory address, which reabsorbs or reintegrates the speaker, thereby abolishing the sense of absence and loss. The 'conversation poem' thus 'acknowledge[s] a dichotomy between subject and object', only to then 'transcend [it] through an act of vision that fuses imagination and its object'. Reading the closing address to Dorothy, Rajan notes that the poem shifts at this point to a form of writing that acts 'not as written text but as living communication' (1980: 213). In turning to the 'conversation poem', then, Wordsworth implicitly aligns himself with a tradition that values oral over written language. As I demonstrated in the previous chapter, recourse to the oral is predominantly associated with the attempt to create a language that is inseparable from notions of presence and origin. Wordsworth's adoption of an oral mode of discourse in the final section of 'Tintern Abbey' accordingly suggests to Rajan that, by its conclusion, the poem seems to have 'free[d] itself from ... ambiguit[y]' (1980: 219).

The ending of 'Tintern Abbey' is, however, more complex than this interpretation might suggest. The poem closes with a benediction, which seeks to confer on Dorothy the consolations of memory that the poet himself has discovered and revealed. The speaker hopes that in future years:

> If solitude, or fear, or pain, or grief,
> Should be thy portion, with what healing thoughts
> Of tender joy wilt thou remember me,
> And these my exhortations! Nor, perchance,
> If I should be, where I no more can hear
> Thy voice, nor catch from thy wild eyes these gleams
> Of past existence, wilt thou then forget
> That on the banks of this delightful stream
> We stood together ...
>   Nor wilt thou then forget,

That after many years of wanderings, many years
Of absence, these steep woods and lofty cliffs,
And this green pastoral landscape, were to me
More dear, both for themselves, and for thy sake.

(ll. 144–52; 156–60)

Taking this passage at face value, Mary Warnock argues that the poem concludes with a straightforward assertion that '[t]he capacity to retain memory images ... is a peculiar blessing' (1987: 87). Geoffrey Strickland rightly contends, however, that 'this is not quite perhaps what Wordsworth is saying'. He goes on to note that Wordsworth 'is not stating a truth or reaching a conclusion but uttering what he himself, in the conclusion of "Tintern Abbey", calls a "prayer"' (1988: 396). The implication of the closing lines is that for Dorothy, too, the physical presence of the landscape will one day be absent, available only in the form of a recovered image or re-presentation. Although Wordsworth hopes that the future recollection of the present scene will protect her from a variety of imagined or projected misfortunes, this hope seems somewhat precarious in the face of the repeated 'forget', which is placed prominently at the ends of the lines. 'Tintern Abbey', then, does not articulate in its closing lines a victory over memory, but rather indicates, in spite of the conscious elevation of its language, the fragility of memory's consolations.

Some years after her initial reading, Tilottama Rajan significantly returned to her interpretation of 'Tintern Abbey' as a 'conversation poem'. In her later reading, she is primarily concerned with the notion of community that is implied within the poem. Like other examples of the genre, 'Tintern Abbey' dramatizes the ideal of a closed network of circulation; Wordsworth creates an intimate, private community, which comprises Dorothy and the speaker, and together they share a privileged insight and wisdom which, Wordsworth hopes, will protect them from the varieties of harm that others can inflict:

And this prayer I make,
Knowing that Nature never did betray
The heart that loved her; 'tis her privilege,

Through all the years of this our life, to lead
From joy to joy: for she can so inform
The mind that is within us, so impress
With quietness and beauty, and so feed
With lofty thoughts, that neither evil tongues,
Rash judgements, nor the sneers of selfish men,
Nor greetings where no kindness is, nor all
The dreary intercourse of daily life,
Shall e'er prevail against us, or disturb
Our cheerful faith that all which we behold
Is full of blessings.

(ll. 122–35)

As Rajan points out, however, 'Tintern Abbey', although distinguished from the *Lyrical Ballads*, is nevertheless printed by Wordsworth in dialogue with it. The focus of this collection is on the inclusion of people from 'all walks' (1990: 136) of rural life and, read together, the poems form a dialogue or conversation across a sympathetic community. Across the poems, then, individuals who differ in terms of age, class, gender, or occupation talk to each other and are bound together by the common language that they share. An ordinary experience from the poet's life, the experience of returning to and surveying a landscape, is thus placed beside experiences in the lives of other ordinary people. Wordsworth's publication of 'Tintern Abbey' therefore opens up important questions concerning the relation between private and public experience, and the bounds or limits of individualism. At the close of the previous section, I pointed out that, for Ferguson, 'romantic memory' is invariably tied to the claims of the collective. To what extent, then, can we read 'Tintern Abbey' as a poem that, for all that it seems to celebrate a closed and private community, is also concerned with the claims of others upon the self?

Following the argument advanced by Thomas Pfau in *Romantic Moods*, I would like to consider Wordsworth's poem in the broader context of the years between 1793 and 1815, an era of unremitting warfare and unprecedented legal, political, and cultural change. Read against this backdrop, Pfau contends, the central dilemma articulated within Wordsworth's poetry of this period becomes how to assimilate the rapid and pervasive historical transformations that were occurring, and which confounded available explanatory frameworks. Pfau highlights, in particular, the marked turn to lyric and pastoral writing in this period, which famously characterized Wordsworth's poetry, but was also evident in the work of many of his British and European contemporaries. Pfau notes that the seeming tranquillity and composure of such writing is, in fact, 'painstakingly elaborated so as to shelter its speakers from the impinging knowledge of ... a historical world so entropic and volatile as to preclude its timely comprehension' (2005: 21). Lyric poetry thus represented a 'virtual zone of safety', which allowed historical self-knowledge to unfold in an oblique, and therefore manageable, form (2005: 215). In this context, then, Wordsworth's poetry can be seen to explore what it means to inhabit a world in which historical change happens too soon, too quickly to fully absorb, so that its consequences can only become apparent after the fact.

Wordsworth notably structures 'Tintern Abbey' around a movement of return that seeks to fix an earlier experience in its place, to absorb and transform a former event by making it happen again. The poem opens, as Bromwich has remarked (1998: 77), by repeating, and impressing upon us, the date of Wordsworth's earlier visit to Tintern: 'Five years have passed; five summers, with the length / Of five long winters!' (ll. 1–2). This takes Wordsworth back to the time just after his return from France; his first visit to Tintern, the poem therefore implies by its very repetition, was too soon after the hectic and bloody events of the Revolution for him to be able to make sense of his experience. The landscape around Tintern nonetheless seems to have assumed a particular significance for him at that time, because it sustained him against the terrors to which he had been exposed in France. He thus fled to the landscape from 'something', unnamed and perhaps unnameable, that was for him a source of 'dread' (l. 72). Likewise, he particularly values the 'soft inland murmur' (l. 4) of the waters around Tintern; the Wye valley is, indeed, as Bromwich points out, almost 'as far inland as he can get in his native land, and as far as possible from France' (1998: 81). Wordsworth returns in the poem, then, to a place that is primarily associated with putting the subject of France out of his mind, leaving it safely behind. In his perceptive reading, however, Bromwich contends that the poem demonstrates to us, through its detailed description of the landscape, the gradual process of absorbing and transforming the past: 'One has a strong sense of Wordsworth sorting out the objects of the eye, slowly connecting each with each, as if bound by the laws of an unfamiliar but precious therapy' (1998: 86). Wordsworth performs a mental work that is consoling, but his consolation ultimately remains profoundly uncertain. The date of the poem, and of his return to Tintern, is specified in the title of the poem as July 13, 1798, the eve of the sixth anniversary of Bastille Day. As Bromwich notes, then, Wordsworth's act of memory operates in the 'careful distance ... that separates 13 July from 14 July, or five years ago from six years ago' (1998: 89). The violent shock of the Revolution is thus not wholly occluded from the poem; rather, it is registered obliquely and hesitantly. The past, it seems, does not exist as knowledge, to be straightforwardly elaborated, but must be staged instead in the form of a complex dialectical process between past and present. This process at once defends against the return of a memory that is seen to be both threatening and overwhelming, and paradoxically provides the very grounds for its re-emergence and realization.

'Tintern Abbey' therefore dramatizes Wordsworth's return to a landscape that he had formerly visited shortly after his return from France, when he was unable to properly absorb the implications of what he had encountered there. Drawing on Pfau's work, I have argued that the poem seeks to fashion a new aesthetic that can convey, albeit indirectly, the unprecedented force of the events of the Revolution. Perhaps unsurprisingly, given that the poem is explicitly discussed by Ferguson, 'Tintern Abbey' also exemplifies 'romantic memory' by reflecting upon, in addition to simply recalling, past experience. The poem is, in addition, intimately concerned with the necessary intertwining of the self with others. Even though Wordsworth seeks to escape into the seclusion of the pastoral landscape, his poem documents the persistent press of public events on his private life. Throughout the *Lyrical Ballads*, he recognizes that no-one, however peripheral they may seem to the economic and social upheavals of the revolutionary and early-capitalist era, could escape being implicated in its history. In registering his inevitable connection to historical events that he can neither fully comprehend nor convey, Wordsworth's writing assumes a testimonial function, speaking for the ways in which we are all personally bound to a broader public or collective history. It is in this sense, then, that 'Tintern Abbey' can properly be said to belong to the *Lyrical Ballads*, for Wordsworth bases his poem on an assumption that the experiences of the ordinary self are relevant to his readers, and he speaks with eloquent authority as a result.

Peter Fritzsche has recently noted that there was a prolific and unprecedented outpouring of the literature of self-reflection, which was inaugurated by Rousseau, across Europe and America in the early years of the nineteenth century. Faced with the ongoing dislocations of revolution and war, there was an increasing sense at this time that the ordinary life stories of individual writers reflected, and were of interest to, the lives of their readers. This was, Fritzsche contends, precisely because they involved 'the reconsideration of those lives in the light of historical change' (2004: 82). Wordsworth's writing thus contributes to a broader investment in the literature of the self, which provided, in the aftermath of the Revolution, an important context in which individuals were able to re-evaluate the significance of their lives and declare their own experiences as of concern to a broader reading public. Richard Terdiman argues, in a similar vein, that the turn of the nineteenth century witnessed, particularly in France, an intensification of relation with the past, which amounted to what he terms a 'memory crisis' (1993: 4). In the following chapter, I seek to address the impact of this 'crisis' on the conceptualization and representation of memory from the late nineteenth century. I will argue, in particular, that there is, in late-nineteenth- and twentieth-century accounts of memory, a continued emphasis on the individual. Particular importance came to be attached to the activity of narrating the self, most famously in the forms of Freud's 'talking cure' and Proust's monumental autobiographical novel *A la recherche du temps perdu* [In Search of Lost Time]. In this sense, then, the Enlightenment and Romantic linking of memory and the self, which has been the main focus of this chapter, was carried forward into the late nineteenth and twentieth centuries and became central to a key strand of the 'late-modern' discourse of memory. As we will see in the remainder of the volume, however, the prioritizing of individual experience that runs through Freud, Bergson, and Proust to contemporary trauma theory is countered by an alternative strand of thinking about memory, which seeks to elaborate a more social, cultural, or collective form of remembering.

3

INVOLUNTARY MEMORIES

My central focus in this chapter is on the relation between memory and late modernity. Typically, an emergent anxiety regarding memory is dated to the late nineteenth and early twentieth centuries, and is linked to accelerated processes of modernization, the impact of the industrial revolution, and the advent of technological warfare. These factors, as Walter Benjamin has pointed out, destroyed traditional communities and ways of life, and they also gave rise to the traumatic symptoms which became the focus of Sigmund Freud's science of psycho-analysis. The late-nineteenth-century foregrounding of memory is often seen, in turn, as distinct from the late-twentieth-century 'memory boom'. Between the two lie the totalitarian atrocities perpetrated under Nazism and Communism. The horrors of the Holocaust, in particular, are understandably accorded central importance in many accounts of contemporary memory studies. The Holocaust has thus commonly been seen to mark a radical break in memorial consciousness, giving rise to concerns about the very possibility of representation and remembrance, and producing a concentrated focus on the traumatic memories of those who survived its terrors.

In what follows, I would like to trace an alternative narrative trajectory which centres on the concept of a prolonged late-modern 'memory crisis'. This notion is indebted to Richard Terdiman's incisive analysis of a 'long nineteenth-century' memory crisis, which originated in the cultural and historical dislocations of the French Revolution (1993: 5). My reading of Wordsworth's 'Tintern Abbey' at the close of the preceding chapter argued that the unprecedented social, economic, and legal changes in the years of, and immediately following, the Revolution could be regarded as the advent of a particularly intense preoccupation with the functioning of memory. For Terdiman, too, the Revolution marked a fundamental disruption of memory, so that it came to seem at once lost and overly present: 'Beginning in the early nineteenth century, we could say that disquiet about memory crystallized around the perception of two principal disorders: *too little memory*, and *too much*' (1993: 14; original emphasis). Perceptions that memory had become pathological generated both anxious concern and intense reflection, and both of these processes have arguably continued into the present.

My analysis also draws on Susannah Radstone's contention that the late-twentieth-century fascination with memory marks not so much a break with nineteenth-century concerns as a 'deepening' of them; for her, the ambivalent relations to community, tradition, and the past, which emerged in the nineteenth century, 'bear yet more forcefully upon the late twentieth century' (2000: 6). Radstone recognizes the continuities between nineteenth- and twentieth-century conceptions of memory, suggesting that the fundamental problems with which they are concerned remain the same. However, she also allows for differentiation between them in suggesting that changed cultural, social, and technological processes have, if anything, intensified the pressures on memory in the late twentieth century. Radstone also, rightly, recognizes the centrality of the Holocaust to 'memory's resonances in contemporary culture' (2000: 6); although she does not position it as a radical break or caesura in memory studies, setting nineteenth-century concerns with memory apart from our own, she does nevertheless acknowledge its undoubted and profound impact on the field. My own writing in this chapter seeks to trace a 'deepening' concern with specifically traumatic forms of memory from the nineteenth century to the present, through readings of Sigmund Freud, Henri Bergson, Marcel Proust, Cathy Caruth, and Charlotte Delbo. I will argue that some of the fiercest controversies currently surrounding traumatic memory are fundamentally imbricated in nineteenth-century issues and debates, thereby indicating an underlying continuity of thought. I also thereby suggest, however, that the late-modern 'memory crisis', in its intensifying preoccupation with the tenacious hold of the past over the present, remains essentially ongoing and unresolved.

As an initial illustration of the ways in which the nineteenth-century memory crisis can be said to continue into the late twentieth century, even as its concerns are differently inflected, I would like to turn briefly to Friedrich Nietzsche's celebrated essay 'On the Uses and Disadvantages of History for Life', which formed the second of his *Untimely Meditations* published in 1874. For Terdiman, the nineteenth-century memory crisis entailed that memory arose unbidden and in forms that seemed increasingly intrusive and malignant. This, he argues, is 'the disease of *too much memory* ... Under such conditions, individual subjectivity is overwhelmed by the persistence of the past and comes to seem dominated, indeed possessed by it' (1993: 84; original emphasis). Nietzsche assumes particular significance for Terdiman as the philosopher who most acutely articulates this sense of memory as a burden. Comparing man to the grazing cattle, Nietzsche envies the animals their happiness which is based on their instantaneous and continual forgetting: 'for [them] every moment really dies, sinks back into night and fog and is extinguished for ever'. For man, by contrast, the accumulated weight of the past threatens to crush him entirely: '[he] braces himself against the great and ever greater pressure of what is past: it pushes him down or bends him sideways, it encumbers his steps as a dark, invisible burden which he would like to disown' (1997: 61). Nietzsche famously revolts against this almost intolerable burden, offering in his essay a defence of forgetting. Specifically, he recommends the forgetting of history, which becomes more and more complex over time so that the sheer task of remembrance causes the historian to lose the ability to act and to live. It is not only the historian who is weakened by the burden of the past, however; for Nietzsche, *everyone* in the nineteenth century has succumbed to the malady of history. Thus, Nietzsche concludes his essay by observing that active or willed forgetting is as important as remembering, if health and happiness are to be attained: '*the unhistorical and the historical are necessary in equal measure for the health of an individual, of a people and of a culture*' (1997: 63; original emphasis).

At the opening of *The Unbearable Lightness of Being* (1984), Milan Kundera returns to Nietzsche's meditations on history and forgetting. Like Nietzsche, Kundera is troubled by the weight of the past and the excessive burden of remembrance that it imposes upon him: 'the weight of unbearable responsibility lies heavy on every move we make' (1984: 4). As Edward Casey notes, the central question with which Kundera is concerned therefore remains essentially unchanged from the nineteenth century: if there is too much memory, Casey observes, 'what will we choose – the way of remembering or the way of forgetting?' (1987: 4). As Kundera continues, however, he notably formulates a contrary response to that chosen by Nietzsche:

> But is heaviness truly deplorable and lightness splendid?
> The heaviest of burdens crushes us, we sink beneath it, it pins us to the ground. But in the love poetry of every age, the woman longs to be weighed down by the man's body. The heaviest of burdens is therefore simultaneously an image of life's most intense fulfilment. The heavier the burden, the closer our ties come to the earth, the more real and truthful they become.
>
> (Kundera 1984: 4–5)

In Kundera, the lightness of forgetting no longer seems 'splendid' but spurious: although it can lighten the burden of our existence, it can also disburden us in more troubling ways, leaving us feeling 'insignificant' and only 'half real' (1984: 5). The weight of memory, by contrast, may embroil us but it also connects us both to others and to reality itself. For both Nietzsche in the late nineteenth century and Kundera in the late twentieth century, the past is thus experienced as an overwhelming and crushing burden. Nietzsche is able to counter this weight, even if only in theory, by proposing the 'lightness' of forgetting; for Kundera, however, remembering seems to assume a crucial moral and ethical dimension. To remember may be a crushing and painful activity but it is also a 'responsibility'; he implies that to actively forget the sufferings of the recent past would be more truly 'unbearable' than to carry their weight within him.

My pairing of Nietzsche and Kundera has sought to indicate, albeit briefly, the 'deepening' or intensification of the concerns of the nineteenth century in late-twentieth-century conceptions of memory. Both writers are fundamentally concerned with the overwhelming presence of the past, the weight of tradition, and the relation of the individual to the community, although these pressures are inflected differently over time. In what follows, I aim to trace in more detail than has been possible here the vicissitudes of the prolonged and ongoing late-modern 'memory crisis'. My analysis attends to the elaboration across a number of philosophical and literary writers of an urgent sense of disruption in relation to the past, which paradoxically renders memory at once elusive and overly intrusive. In addition, I argue that, in the very process of reconceptualizing and refiguring memory, many of these writers also self-consciously construct and reflect upon their own understanding of, and relationship to, what can broadly be termed the 'modern'.

FREUD'S 'MYSTIC WRITING PAD'

In the classic dictionary of psychoanalytical terms, Jean Laplanche and J.-B. Pontalis' *The Language of Psycho-Analysis* (1988), there is no entry for 'memory'. The concepts of 'remembrance' and 'forgetting' are likewise absent from the volume. This gap does not, however, permit us to conclude that Freud was uninterested in such issues. Rather, as David Farrell Krell has noted, memory lies at the very core of the psychoanalytic project: 'psychoanalysis takes memory to be the source of both the *malady* with which it is concerned and the *therapy* it proffers' (1990: 106; original emphasis). In addition to his elaboration of psychoanalysis as a scientific treatment of memory, Freud himself was apparently capable of extraordinary feats of recall, and he impressed on the practising analyst the need to take notes only after the therapeutic session was over, when the conversation should be recorded from memory. Harald Weinrich observes that Freud took a keen 'interest in mnemotechnics' (2004: 132), while Terdiman goes so far as to suggest that psychoanalysis can be considered as the last great flowering of the form: 'Psychoanalysis is our culture's last Art of Memory' (1993: 240). In the discussion that follows, I will suggest that Freud drew on a specifically Platonic strand of classical mnemonics, returning to the Socratic dialogue for his formulation of the 'talking cure' and to Plato's image of the 'wax tablet' for his concept of the unconscious. Nonetheless, Terdiman's analysis of Freud is concerned less to establish the classical antecedents of his thinking than to locate him at the heart of the nineteenth-century memory crisis. In this context, Terdiman argues, Freud brings a particular density of attention to his analysis of memory, and specifically to his understanding of the power of the past over the present. Psychoanalysis, then, 'exacerbates [the memory crisis] to its point of greatest intensity and places it in its most perspicuous light' (1993: 242–3). From the very origins of his work, Freud thus focused on precisely those moments when the past called out for attention in the form of symptoms, dreams, and linguistic slips. Faced with these encrypted riddles, which remained oblivious to their own origins, Freud recognized that what seemed inexplicable in the present could be readily interpreted by invoking the presence of a painful, and hence hitherto unacknowledged, memory. Prior to Freud, Terdiman points out, the extent and power of memory had never before been 'conceived as so ubiquitous or so sovereign' (1993: 247).

'*Hysterics suffer mainly from reminiscences*' (*SE* II: 7; original emphasis). In this famous formulation from *Studies on Hysteria*, originally published in 1895, Freud unequivocally linked the hysterical symptom to a buried memory, which usually referred to an event in childhood. Although the memory itself was unavailable to the patient, except in the highly condensed form of the symptom, its influence nevertheless persisted into the present. The repressed memory, Freud argued, 'acts like a foreign body which long after its entry must continue to be regarded as an agent that is still at work'. The analyst was able to bring to light the memory of the event with the aid of hypnosis; once the patient had put the memory into words, at the same time as closely reproducing its accompanying affect, its baneful influence was entirely dissipated: 'each individual hysterical symptom immediately and permanently disappeared' (*SE* II: 6). In *Studies on Hysteria*, Freud tentatively gestured towards sexuality as an underlying cause of the hysterical symptom: 'in so far as one can speak of determining causes which lead to the *acquisition* of neuroses, their aetiology is to be looked for in *sexual* factors' (*SE* II: 257; original emphasis). It was not until the following year, however, in his 1896 paper 'Heredity and the Aetiology of the Neuroses', that he explicitly stated a connection between hysteria and the memory of childhood sexual abuse:

> The event of which the subject has retained an unconscious memory is *a precocious experience of sexual relations with actual excitement of the genitals, resulting from sexual abuse committed by another person; and the period of life* at which this fatal event takes place is *earliest youth –* the years up to the age of eight or ten, before the child has reached sexual maturity.
>
> (Freud *SE* III: 152; original emphasis)

The hysterical symptom, then, preserves the memory of one or more events of sexual abuse in the patient's past life, typically from early childhood, events of which the patient remains consciously unaware. The past with which the analyst is concerned is thus conceived of by Freud as essentially static and unchanging; the task of psychoanalysis consists, he asserts, in 'the unlocking of a locked door' (*SE* II: 283). Once the obstacle or resistance to remembering has been removed, the past is simply recovered or uncovered in its original, intact form.

Within a few years of asserting the cause of hysteria to lie in his patients' memories of childhood seduction, Freud grew sceptical of the validity and reliability of childhood memories. In his 1899 essay 'Screen Memories', he argues that apparently vivid memories of early childhood, which are concerned with everyday and indifferent events, often refer to an entirely different set of experiences which are of far greater affective significance.

Childhood memories are characteristically 'screened' by mnemic images, which bear some point of analogy to the original event but at the same time disguise and displace it. Freud concludes 'Screen Memories' by noting that it is doubtful 'whether we have any memories at all *from* our childhood: memories *relating to* our childhood may be all that we possess'. Although childhood memories seem to show us our early years as they were, they can in reality only reveal them as they appeared at the time of remembering; in this sense, then, 'childhood memories did not *emerge*; they were *formed* at that time' (*SE* III: 322; original emphasis). In *The Psychopathology of Everyday Life*, from 1901, Freud again reiterates this point: 'in the so-called earliest childhood memories we possess not the genuine memory trace but a later revision of it, a revision which may have been subjected to the influences of a variety of later psychical forces' (*SE* VI: 47–8). Here, then, Freud articulates a version of memory in which the past no longer resides in the original impressions, but in the process of remembering itself. The past is no longer inert and passive, but is powerfully reshaped in and through the concerns of the present. The delayed action of remembering, in other words, allows the past to develop, to evolve along with changing circumstances over time. In the face of this more complex and shifting memory process, the task of the analyst is no longer one of straightforward recovery but of reconstruction, which provides a narrative of the past not as it was but as it might have been.

Freud's shift in the conceptualization of memory led to a corresponding development in the methodology of psychoanalysis itself. Freud quickly abandoned the technique of hypnosis, which aimed at recovering the buried or repressed memory, in favour of the 'talking cure'. As he outlines in his 1914 paper 'Remembering, Repeating and Working Through', this method no longer focuses on 'bring[ing] a particular moment ... into focus'; rather, the analyst studies 'whatever is present for the time being on the surface of the patient's mind' (*SE* XII: 147). Remembering is thus conceived as an activity which takes place in and is fundamentally shaped by the present. In the analytic session, the patient experiences her past as 'something real and contemporary' (*SE* XII: 152), because she powerfully acts out former attitudes and behaviours.

The analyst is able to intervene by bringing to the patient's open reminiscing or transferential feelings his different memories and associations, which means that the past will not simply be repeated or reproduced but subverted and undone. The new focus of analysis is on allowing the past to slowly develop or evolve, and to be revised in line with the changed circumstances of the patient's present life both within and beyond the analytic session. In place of the instantaneous and permanent disappearance of the symptom under hypnosis, Freud accordingly places emphasis at the close of 'Remembering, Repeating and Working Through' on the 'arduous task' of analysis, which demands a considerable investment of time and patience on the part of both analyst and analysand (*SE* XII: 155).

Particularly striking in Freud's notion of the 'talking cure' is the close relation that he posits between recollection and dialogue. Although the patient is involved in producing a narrative of the self, remembrance is only possible for Freud by way of a detour in which the expression of memory passes through an interlocutor, namely the analyst. In this aspect of his work, as Edward Casey has noted, Freud draws on a specifically Platonic strand of thinking:

> Plato's doctrine of recollection ... shows considerable affinity with Freud's view of memory. Much as abreactive recollection becomes possible only through dialectical confrontation in psychotherapy, philosophical recollection or *anamnesis* arises after a process of dialectical cross-examination (*elenchus*).
>
> (Casey 1987: 302; original emphasis)

As in Plato's *Meno*, then, Freudian memory is based on a dialectical process which elicits recollection, bringing forth that which the patient has long forgotten ever having known. The 'talking cure' can thus be seen to originate in and refer back to the classical form of the Socratic dialogue. Implicit in this Platonic model is the notion of the interlocutor as teacher, with a privileged access to the contents of memory. In this context, Allan Young has observed of the development of psychoanalysis: 'Without the intervention of an expert, the owner of a "parasitic" memory remained unaware of its content and ignorant that it influenced aspects of his life' (1997: 4). However, Young risks overstating here the passivity of the analysand in the analytic process: although the analyst is necessary as a catalyst to remembrance, it is the patient who actively 'discovers' the memory and/or works it through. As Casey notes, Freud also inherits from Plato 'a ... tradition of "activism"', in which 'recollection takes place as a search'. Importantly, however, Casey goes on to point out that Freud and Plato are curiously aligned in the history of memory studies, for each thinker stresses both activism and passivism in their work, although the two traditions have otherwise 'remained remarkably independent of each other from Periclean Athens to the present day' (1987: 15). Passivism thus enters Freudian psychoanalysis through another key Platonic motif, the metaphor of the wax tablet, which provides a model for the unconscious and reintroduces into his work the notion of memory as imprinting. In the remainder of this section, I therefore intend to elaborate in more detail the Freudian model of the unconscious, in order to demonstrate the ways in which this aspect of his work both contradicts and undercuts the tendency in psychoanalysis towards revision and representation, that has formed the focus of my discussion so far.

In his essay of 1915, 'The Unconscious', Freud refutes from the outset attempts to locate memory neurologically. In nineteenth-century medical discourse, a voluminous literature had arisen from attempts to map memory-storage locations onto the anatomy of the brain. For Freud, however, '[e]very attempt to ... discover a localization of mental processes, every endeavour to think of ideas as stored up in nerve-cells and of excitations as travelling along nerve-fibres, has miscarried completely' (SE XIV: 174). Such a conception of memory is, in the words of Terdiman, 'prosaically realist' and relies on a model of storage, a fixing of the inscription which implies that 'what went into the brain can come out unchanged' (1993: 264). In place of the excessive literalism of his contemporaries, Freud turns instead to a topographical model of the psyche, which refers 'not to anatomical localities but to regions in the mental apparatus, wherever they may be situated in the body' (SE XIV: 175). He distinguishes, in the first instance, between the conscious (system Cs.) and the unconscious (system *Ucs.*); between these two, and acting as a censor for the contents of the unconscious before they reach consciousness, is the preconscious (system *Pcs.*). Consciousness is the place where external stimuli are registered; it is not therefore an appropriate repository for memory, for this function would soon limit the capacity of consciousness to receive fresh excitations. The unconscious therefore becomes for Freud the place where memory resides. Crucially, Freud conceives of the unconscious as timeless: its contents, he explains, are 'not ordered temporally' and, more importantly, they are 'not altered by the passage of time' (*SE* XIV: 187). By implication, then, once memory has been inscribed in the system *Ucs.*, it is immutable and unchangeable, not open to influence or revision from outside.

Although memory is retained in the unconscious, it becomes available only when it crosses the topographical boundary surrounding the system *Ucs.* At this point in his argument, Freud notably hesitates: does the process of transition from the unconscious to the conscious involve a change of state, implying that the memory can be removed from the unconscious; or is there a second inscription of the memory, a new and separate registration of it in the system *Cs.*, suggesting that it exists simultaneously at two different levels of the psyche? Significantly, Freud prefers the second conceptual model, which reinforces the permanence of unconscious memory traces. He argues that the inscription of memory in the conscious belongs to the system of language; it comprises 'the presentation of the thing plus the presentation of the word belonging to it'. In the unconscious, however, memory consists of 'the presentation of the thing alone' (*SE* XIV: 201); it is not susceptible to language, and remains radically and irreducibly alien. In Freud's model, then, as Terdiman explains, although the unconscious provides 'output' to the rest of the psyche, it is itself 'inaccessible to input, moderation, modulation, or diminution' (1993: 284). This entails in the first instance, as I have indicated above, the return to a passive model of memory. Once laid down in the unconscious, memory is not subject to revision or retranscription, except at another layer of the psyche which does not affect its original registration. In addition, however, the impossibility of removing from the unconscious those memories which are most toxic and harmful to us poses a radical and seemingly insoluble problem for psychoanalysis itself. If memories are inexorably and changelessly fixed, then the notion of the 'cure' becomes fatally compromised. The implication arising out of Freud's 1915 study is that the symptom, which originates from the preconscious or conscious retranscription of the memory, may be modified or removed, but the underlying cause of the symptom, the unconscious memory itself, cannot finally be eliminated.

In 'Beyond the Pleasure Principle', published in 1920, Freud elaborates further on his topographical model. Modifying his original conception, he relocates the function of registration from the conscious to the preconscious. Imagining a living organism in its most simplified form, 'an undifferentiated vesicle of a substance that is susceptible to stimulation', Freud conjectures that the surface of this organism which has direct contact with the external world will be differentiated, and will 'serve as an organ for receiving stimuli'. In the course of time, the unceasing impact of external energies will permanently modify this surface, so that it forms a 'crust' which has been thoroughly 'baked through' by the stimulation to which it has been exposed (*SE* XVIII: 26). The surface, which represents the system *Cs.*, is accordingly capable of no further modification; rather than acting as a receptive layer, it works to protect against stimuli and to shield the receptive surface which lies below, the system *Pcs.*, from being overwhelmed by excitations. In transposing the function of the conscious to the preconscious, Freud emphasizes that the principal aim of the psychic apparatus is to maintain at the lowest possible level the quantities of excitation from outside. The external world is conceived as an overwhelming and threatening environment, 'charged with the most powerful energies'. Without a protective shield, the organism would be 'killed by the stimulation'; instead, the outermost surface of the system *Cs.* acts as a 'special envelope or membrane', allowing the energies to pass into the system *Pcs.* 'with only a fragment of their original intensity' (*SE* XVIII: 27). Trauma arises when a stimulus is so powerful that it breaks through the protective shield and floods the underlying mental apparatus. The primary concerns of the individual are then to retrospectively master the amounts of stimulus which have broken in, and to repair the breach that has been made in the outer system *Cs*. For Freud, 'preparedness for anxiety' constitutes the vital mode of defence against trauma (*SE* XVIII: 31); accordingly, the traumatized individual seeks to establish these mechanisms of preparedness after the fact, through repetitive dreams and behaviours which build up anxiety by returning him to the original fright.

A few years later, in 1924, Freud published a brief meditation on memory, which he entitled 'A Note upon the "Mystic Writing Pad"'. This work is important for our purposes because it summarizes the topography of the psyche in terms of processes of inscription, and it is here that Freud refers back to the metaphor of the wax tablet in defining the unconscious. The essay begins by assessing the available models of writing apparatus as analogies for the memory process. The central problem, as Freud outlines it, is that these apparatuses capture either the faculty of retention or that of reception, but they fail to articulate both. Thus writing in ink on paper 'will preserve intact any note made on it for an indefinite length of time', so that it has excellent retentive capacities, but 'the receptive capacity of the writing-surface is soon exhausted' as the sheet is filled. Writing with chalk on a blackboard, on the contrary, means that the surface is infinitely receptive, for 'the notes upon [it] can be destroyed as soon as they cease to interest me'. This is, however, at the expense of retention, for in wiping out the notes that are no longer useful, 'I cannot preserve a permanent trace' (*SE* XIX: 227). Freud accordingly turns to the newly marketed 'Mystic Writing Pad', which represents for him a more faithful model of the psyche because of its ability to combine both functions. The Mystic Pad, he explains, comprises a slab of wax which is overlaid with a thin transparent sheet. The sheet itself consists of two layers which can be detached from each other: the upper layer is a transparent piece of celluloid, while the lower layer is made of thin waxed paper. To use the pad, one writes with a pointed stylus on the double covering sheet that rests upon the wax; in this sense, Freud explains with a backward glance to Plato, '[i]t is a return to the ancient method of writing on tablets of clay or wax' (*SE* XIX: 229). The writing is visible on the surface of the celluloid; if one wishes to erase what one has written, however, it is necessary only to raise the double covering

sheet from the wax slab and the pad is once again clear of writing. Although the waxed paper beneath the celluloid records the
writing just as clearly as the celluloid covering, Freud explains
that the thin paper would easily be torn by the stylus, and the
layer of celluloid thus acts as a 'protective sheath ... to keep off
injurious effects from without'. Here, then, the Mystic Pad imi-
tates the tendency of the psychical apparatus to allow through the
lowest possible level of external excitation, for the outer layer of
celluloid, representing the system $Cs.$, acts as a shield to protect
the receptive layer beneath. In addition to this, however, the
underlying wax slab retains a 'permanent trace' of what was written;
the inscription remains on its surface, even after the contact with
the paper has been brought to an end, and it is clearly 'legible in
suitable lights' (SE XIX: 230). The wax slab thus comes to represent
the system $Ucs.$, and it is unequivocal from Freud's description
that the memories which are retained there are ineradicable and
cannot be removed or erased. In this sense, then, the Mystic Pad
offers a model for the dual function of the psychical apparatus, for
it is capable of both retention and infinite reception. Freud's
argument thus suggests, as Krell has indicated, that the Mystic
Pad is no 'mere regression' to the 'primitive style' of the wax
tablet (1990: 154), for it offers a more complex layering of
inscription. However, Freud's model of the unconscious notably
contradicts this implied advance from Plato, by merely replicating
the traditional metaphor of the wax tablet. Just as Plato regarded
the writing on the soul to be an incorruptible copy of eternal
truths, so Freud conceives the inscriptions on the unconscious to be
immutable and timeless. The therapeutic ambitions of psychoanalysis, which depend on a more mobile and temporary registration
of the memory trace, thus threaten to be undone by the model of
writing which underpins Freud's conceptual apparatus, and which
becomes explicit in his description of the 'Mystic Writing Pad'.

As Jacques Derrida has convincingly demonstrated in 'Freud
and the Scene of Writing', his celebrated analysis of 'A Note upon
the "Mystic Writing Pad"', Freud increasingly turns to the model
of writing in his theorization of the psyche. Derrida's own reading
of the 'Note' accords special privilege to the materiality of the
Mystic Pad itself. Paying particular attention to Freud's comparison

of the Mystic Pad to the wax tablet, Derrida notes that the process of writing with which Freud is concerned is incisional; unlike writing on paper or on a blackboard, which represents marking a flat plane or surface, Freud's Mystic Pad has both depth and interiority. An important implication of this model is that psychical processes, like the act of inscription, are not straightforwardly localizable: the stratification or layering of the pad means that the inscription is distributed across a number of different surfaces, just as external stimuli are registered at differing levels of the psyche and their violence thereby diminished. Inscription on the psyche, like the writing on the pad, thus does not simply take place once; it requires, as Christopher Johnson succinctly explains, 'a certain repetition that problematizes any assignation of a unitary origin' (1993: 97). Perhaps of more significance for Derrida, however, is the temporal dimension that is implied by the successive layers of the pad, and which offers a particularly interesting analogy to the processes of remembering. The structure of the pad entails that the inscription on the celluloid surface will disappear once its contact with the wax slab has been broken. The permanent trace of the writing can then only be read afterwards, by lifting the upper layers and scrutinizing the surface of the wax beneath. Comparing this to the psychical apparatus, Derrida observes that perception is never present to itself but necessarily operates within a belated form of temporality: '[t]he "perceived" may be read only in the past, beneath perception and after it' (2001a: 282). In the model provided by the Mystic Pad, then, Derrida points out that writing no longer represents a 'horizontal ... chain of signs', but has been refigured by Freud as 'the interruption and restoration of contact between the various depths of psychical levels: the remarkably heterogeneous temporal fabric of psychical work itself' (2001a: 283).

Throughout 'Freud and the Scene of Writing', Derrida repeatedly refers to the Mystic Writing Pad as a machine or instrument. The Mystic Pad is indeed introduced by Freud specifically as a supplement to the activity of remembering: 'If I distrust my memory ... I am able to supplement and guarantee its working by making a note in writing' (SE XIX: 227). Here, then, Freud's conception of writing as an aid to remembering recalls Plato's

Phaedrus, in which writing was seen to act as a useful prompt to recollection but to atrophy the faculty of memory itself. As I discussed in Chapter 1, Derrida argues in 'Plato's Pharmacy' that Plato's opposition in the *Phaedrus* between 'bad' writing, or the script of texts, and 'good writing', or the imprinting of eternal Truths on the soul, is inevitably undone by a principle of contamination, which entails that the two modes of inscription are always already implicated in each other. In 'Freud and the Scene of Writing', Derrida accordingly remarks on the abruptness with which Freud breaks off his analogy between the Mystic Pad and the psyche. Freud thus observes: 'There must come a point at which an analogy between an auxiliary apparatus of this kind and the organ which is its prototype will cease to apply. It is true, too, that once the writing has been erased, the Mystic Pad cannot "reproduce" it from within; it would be a mystic pad indeed if, like our memory, it could accomplish that' (*SE* XIX: 230). For Derrida, this overly hasty conclusion to the discussion, coupled with Freud's assertion that only the writing of the psyche is able to reproduce itself spontaneously, suggests that Freud 'continues, like Plato, to oppose hypomnemic writing and writing *en tei psychei* [on the soul]' (2001a: 286). Derrida proposes that, instead of ending here, Freud should have followed further the implications of his own suggestion of a resemblance between the Mystic Pad and memory, in order to elicit 'the possibility of this machine'. Here, Derrida refers to recent advances in artificial intelligence, which have come to resemble memory more closely than the Mystic Pad could ever do: 'the latter is no doubt infinitely more complex than slate or paper, less archaic than a palimpsest; but, compared to other machines for storing archives, it is a child's toy' (2001a: 286–7).

Viewed in retrospect, then, Freud's Mystic Pad both anticipates and provides a limited model for modern simulations of memory in computers and cybernetics. However, where such instances of artificial memory increasingly confuse the boundaries between natural and artificial, living and mechanical, internal and external, Derrida implies that Freud, like Plato, wished to retain and reinforce such distinctions. Derrida thus positions Freud as limited by his return to Plato's theory of writing as supplement, which leads to his privileging the 'inner' writing of the unconscious over the 'external writing' of script, even as he extends beyond Plato's metaphor of the wax tablet in his complex layering of the psychical apparatus. However, Christopher Johnson crucially notes in this regard that Derrida's reading of psychoanalysis is repeatedly and consistently 'resistant' to Freud's belief in, and repeated assertion of, the indestructibility of unconscious memory (1993: 99). In addition to limiting the therapeutic efficacy of psychoanalysis itself, the permanence or timelessness of unconscious memory thus marks, for Johnson at least, an important 'limit upon Derrida's interpretation of Freud' (1993: 100), a site of interpretative blindness in his text, which thereby fails to register the inherent conservatism of Freud's Platonic gesture in figuring the unconscious as a wax tablet.

Terdiman argues that Freud occupies a central position in relation to the late-modern 'memory crisis', because of his prolonged and intense fascination with the power of the past over the present; I have further contended that the baneful influence of the past becomes particularly acute in Freud's elaboration of the unconscious. In conclusion to this section, then, I would like to briefly question the implications of the permanence of the unconscious memory traces for the possibility of the psychoanalytic 'cure'. I have already noted the therapeutic optimism of Freud's earliest writing, which presumed that the hysterical symptom could be instantaneously and permanently removed. As Krell observes, Freud assumes that 'if the analyst succeeds in restoring remembrance of these events in the patient, the symptoms will vanish like pacified ghosts' (1990: 108). In one of his last essays, however, 'Analysis Terminable and Interminable', which was published in 1937, Freud provided a much more limited vision of what analysis could realistically achieve. Posing the question of what marks the 'end' of an analysis, Freud responds that, in practical terms, the analyst and the patient cease to meet each other because so much repressed material has been brought to consciousness that a repetition of the pathology seems unlikely. However, Freud explicitly refutes the notion of a cure that has 'succeeded in resolving every one of the patient's repressions' (*SE* XXIII: 220). More specifically, Freud argues that although 'transformation is achieved' in the course of the analysis, this is necessarily partial, because 'portions of the old mechanisms remain untouched by the work of analysis' (*SE* XXIII: 229). In this sense, Freud's writing articulates an increasing and cumulative belief that the harmful influences of the past cannot be removed or dissipated at the level of the unconscious. Analysis cannot remove the burden of the past, which we are fated to always carry within us. Nietzsche's willed forgetting is thus not an option that is available to Freud, for we cannot simply 'extinguish' the memory of the past; all of our attempts to do so are, indeed, paradoxically greeted by its more aggressive revival or return. The process of analysis can, however, make the burden of the past more bearable, if only temporarily; even if it cannot exorcize the ghosts that haunt us, it can pacify some of them to some degree. Psychoanalysis, Freud concludes, after a lifetime of developing and practising his 'art of memory', is an 'impossible profession'; like education and government, it is one of the few spheres of activity in which 'one can be sure beforehand of achieving unsatisfying results' (*SE* XXIII: 248).

PROUST'S 'MADELEINE'

In the previous section, I argued that the Freudian unconscious draws on Plato's metaphor of the wax tablet. In doing so, it emphasizes the timeless quality of what has been inscribed there; Casey thus notes that the 'pre-personal sphere of the unconscious' parallels the 'pre-existent state' from which Plato's eternal truths derived (1987: 302). This dimension of Plato's writing also resonates powerfully with the work of two of Freud's contemporaries: Henri Bergson, who elaborated the concept of 'pure memory', and Marcel Proust, who famously developed and celebrated the notion of 'involuntary memory'. Michael Sheringham accordingly notes that 'Plato's *anamnesis*, properly speaking the recollection within this life of eternal forms', can be seen as a 'prototype' of memory in Bergson and Proust, particularly in its contrast with '*memoria*, the generally more mundane faculty elucidated by Aristotle' (1993: 289; original emphasis). This comparison finds its counterpart in the subsequent pairings of 'pure memory' with 'habit memory', and 'involuntary' with 'voluntary' memory; in each instance, Sheringham observes, '[n]ot least of the virtues attributed to the positive form of memory ... is the capacity to transcend its negative avatar, associated with workaday, mechanical remembering and ordinary time'. 'True' memory thus offers 'a conquest or redemption of time' and provides access to 'continuity, unity and permanence' (1993: 289). In this section, I will offer an analysis of these pairings of memory in the work of Bergson and Proust, in addition to addressing the complex and contested question of the relation between the two writers.

Henri Bergson's *Matter and Memory*, published in 1896, argues that memory is not in fact singular but rather combines two different kinds of memories. The first is 'habit memory', which consists in obtaining certain forms of automatic behaviour through repetition. Bergson argues that this form of memory 'accumulates within the body'. Coinciding with the acquisition of sensori-motor functions, it organizes movements as 'a series of mechanisms', which are then stored or retained, ready to respond to new external stimuli with learned or rehearsed reactions (1991: 81–2). Habit memory, as Casey points out, operates with greatest efficacy in a 'twilight consciousness' (1987: 164), in which it remembers how to undertake certain actions, but does not necessarily recollect any particular occasions on which the action was successfully performed in the past. Bergson is somewhat disparaging of the mechanical and automatic functioning of habit memory. Specifically, he criticizes the way that the past relates to the present in this form of remembering. The past can thus be regarded as overwhelming the present, for habit memory reinstates it so completely that it ends up by merely repeating it. In the habitual behaviours of walking or writing, for example, the body's past is simply lived and acted in the present, rather than represented. Nonetheless, Bergson's analysis provides an important recognition of the hitherto overlooked role of the body in modes of remembering. Casey thus observes that Bergson was 'the first philosopher to have devoted concerted attention' to body memory, although he goes on to point out that he wrongly took habit memory to represent 'the whole' of body memory (1987: 147). Bergson therefore fails to take into account its alternative forms and modes; he overlooked traumatic body memory, for example, which manifested itself in hysterical symptoms, and which, as I outlined in the previous section, was concurrently being explored and analysed by Freud.

Bergson's second form of memory, which he regards as 'true memory' (1991: 151), is 'pure memory', which refers to the survival of personal memories in the unconscious. He insists from the outset of *Matter and Memory* on the 'utilitarian character' of the psychical functions, which are 'essentially turned toward action' (1991: 16). The priority of the mental apparatus is to receive and retain those experiences which will be useful in determining future behaviours or responses. Crucial to Bergson's account, however, is the recognition that, although all experiences are retained by memory, only some are of practical value. The brain thus suppresses or inhibits, confines to the unconscious, those memories that seem irrelevant. This level of memory, which is constantly at work beneath our everyday consciousness, appeals to Bergson precisely because of its non-utilitarian dimension. In the unconscious, nothing of the past is forgotten or lost; it 'records, in the form of memory-images, all the events of our daily life as they occur in time; it neglects no detail; it leaves to each fact, each gesture, its place and date' (1991: 81). If habit memory is acquired deliberately and painstakingly through an act of 'will', pure memory is, on the contrary, 'entirely spontaneous', both in its faithful preservation of the past and in its reproduction (1991: 88). It becomes available to us at times when our psychic defences are down, as, for example, in dreams, and it is of value because it represents our point of contact with 'timelessness'. For Bergson, all experiences exist timelessly in the unconscious, because time is a category that is imposed on experience by the habitual, conscious mind. Habitual memory enables us to function by converting the flow of experience into successive units, allowing us to arrange things and events and so to make use of them. The timeless duration of spontaneous memory, on the other hand, offers an alternative form of knowledge, which is associated not with the everyday, active life of practicality, but with a more contemplative life and state.

Bergson's distinction between habit memory and pure memory has often been straightforwardly aligned with Proust's voluntary and involuntary memories. There are undoubtedly points of similarity between the two. For Proust, voluntary memory can only yield to us superficial appearances, and it is therefore accorded the secondary status of Bergson's habit memory. As Warnock points out, there is a certain affinity between the two in Proust's recognition that 'the more purely conventional a memory becomes, so that it can be "called up" or repeated without thought, the less it is capable of bringing us to the truth'. A memory image, particularly a visual image, can thus become worn out with overuse, so that 'the voluntary may, in certain of its aspects, become habitual' (1987: 95). Involuntary memory, on the other hand, grasps the past in its entirety, reviving not only a memory image but related sensations and emotions. It captures something of the spontaneity of pure memory, for it surfaces unexpectedly and cannot be deliberately sought; Samuel Beckett thus observes that it 'chooses its own time and place for the performance of its miracle' (1931: 21). However, Proust repeatedly emphasizes that it also takes a tremendous effort to capture exactly what it is that is being remembered. Thus, although the beginning of the memory sequence occurs spontaneously, it is invariably succeeded by a deliberate and prolonged search for the original experience. Proust's involuntary memory also resonates with the timelessness of pure memory: it offers a way to overcome the gap between past and present and so to achieve, in Warnock's words, 'a universal and timeless understanding of what things are like' (1987: 94). Crucially, however, Proust differs from Bergson in according an entirely different role and value to the body in the process of remembering. If the body is trivial in status for Bergson, associated with the merely mechanical, it is essential to Proust's involuntary memory and ushers in its precise and vivid recollections. Throughout *In Search of Lost Time*, a physical sensation thus acts as the catalyst for involuntary memory: the taste of the madeleine dipped in tea, the sensation of imbalance on unevenly laid cobblestones, the sounds of a spoon striking a plate or of water running through pipes, the touch of a heavily starched napkin brushing the lips. As Julia Kristeva points out, Proustian memory is 'grafted in the actual body of the narrator' (1993: 82); it is, in other words, profoundly and irreducibly physical. Proustian memory therefore bears the traces of Bergson's influence; this is understandable, for not only was Bergson Proust's cousin by marriage, but before the end of 1908 – the year when the plan of *In Search of Lost Time* was fixed, although the text passed through successive alterations and adjustments until Proust's death in 1922 – Proust had also read and annotated *Matter and Memory*. Nonetheless, there are significant differences between the two writers, and it seems worth attending to Proust's own protestations, cited by Jack Jordan, that, while they shared a common interest in memory, 'he would have called his novel "bergsonian" instead of ... "a series of novels of the unconscious" if he had thought that it would have been correct to do so' (2001: 102).

Proust asserts the importance of the physical aspect of remembering from the very outset of *In Search of Lost Time*. As Casey observes, he opens the first volume, *Swann's Way*, by 'ingeniously invert[ing] the usual order of proceeding from the psychical to the physical in matters of memory by showing that the richest route into recollection is through body memory' (1987: 171). Proust thus evokes in his celebrated opening passage the liminal state of awakening. It is at precisely this moment that the narrator's body memory comes effectively into play. Initially, Proust's description seems to evoke Bergson's habit memory, for the body acts to make its confused surroundings customary and familiar, and thereby habitable, by projecting through a series of postures various possible environments, until it is able to identify the room in which the narrator has awakened. The body thus acts as a repository of remembered locations: 'Its memory, the composite memory of its ribs, its knees, its shoulder-blades, offered it a series of rooms in which it had at one time or another slept' (*ISLT* I: 4). Proust makes clear that this habitual aspect of body memory is essential in allowing us to domesticate an initially unfamiliar space, and to feel at home there:

> Habit! that skilful but slow-moving arranger who begins by letting our minds suffer for weeks on end in temporary quarters, but whom our minds are none the less only too happy to discover at last, for without

it, reduced to their own devices, they would be powerless to make any room seem habitable!

(Proust *ISLT* I: 7)

Proust extends beyond this Bergsonian emphasis, however, to suggest that the body can play a crucial role in resurrecting the past. The locations that the body projects thus bring back to the narrator in all their detail the forgotten bedrooms of his past. The body recalls not only when and where he lay sleepless in his childhood bedroom, but also *how* he did so; the narrator's 'stiffened side' thus acts as a 'faithful guardian' of the past in recalling exactly how he used to lie, face to the wall, in his canopied bed at Combray (*ISLT* I: 5). Moreover, the body does not recall one detail in isolation, but the ways in which the various elements of a room are interconnected: the memory of the canopied bed brings in its train the night light in its glass bowl and the marble chimney piece. Although these body memories do not last for more than a few seconds, Proust makes clear that they nevertheless form the prelude to a more sustained act of remembering: 'my memory had been set in motion; as a rule I did not attempt to go to sleep again at once, but used to ... rememb[er] again all the places and people I had known, what I had actually seen of them, what others had told me' (*ISLT* I: 8). Although the resurrection of Combray is usually associated with the 'madeleine', its first revival notably occurs in the opening pages of *Swann's Way*. Proust seems to impress upon his reader, not only through what he explicitly tells us but in the very structure of the novel, that the narrator's body memories provide an essential 'preface' or 'overture' to the work of recollection, which is to follow in the main body of the novel itself.

The famous episode of the 'madeleine', which takes place later in *Swann's Way*, further underlines the importance of the body in the Proustian act of remembrance. As a prelude to the scene, the narrator reflects on his previous attempts to deliberately summon Combray, the world of his childhood, through voluntary memory. Such efforts succeed in recalling only an isolated fragment of the past, centred on the hallway, the staircase, and the passage to his bedroom, 'seen always at the same evening hour, ... detached and solitary against the dark background, the bare minimum of scenery necessary' (*ISLT* I: 50). Voluntary memory is thus of no value as an instrument of evocation; it can only produce a caricature of the past, rather than its true picture. Involuntary memory, in contrast, revives the past in its entirety, resurrecting not only his grandparents' house but the whole of the surrounding area:

> And as in the game wherein the Japanese amuse themselves by filling a porcelain bowl with water and steeping in it little pieces of paper which until then are without character or form, but, the moment they become wet, stretch and twist and take on colour and distinctive shape, become flowers or houses or people, solid and recognisable, so in that moment all the flowers in our garden and in M. Swann's park, and the water-lilies on the Vivonne and the good folk of the village and their little dwellings and the parish church and the whole of Combray and its surroundings, taking shape and solidity, sprang into being, towns and gardens alike, from my cup of tea.
>
> (Proust *ISLT* I: 54–5)

The catalyst to remembrance is the madeleine dipped in lime-blossom tea, which evokes a memory of the ritual that, as a child, the narrator used to perform before church at the house of his aunt, 'the little piece of madeleine which on Sunday mornings at Combray ... when I went to say good morning to her in her bedroom, my aunt Léonie used to give me, dipping it first in her own cup of tea or tisane' (*ISLT* I: 53–4). The memory takes on a sacramental quality, recalling a more intimate and private act of communion between the narrator and his aunt than the official Eucharist that is to follow. More importantly, however, the past is reawakened by the sense of taste, which is, Casey notes, 'the most thoroughly participatory form of body memory' (1987: 252). Again, then, Proust asserts the centrality of the physical to the activity of recollection, and invests it with a weight and significance that seem far removed from Bergson's writing: the smell and taste of things remain poised a long time, 'like souls, remembering, waiting, hoping, amid the ruins of all the rest for their moment; ... and bear unfaltering, in the tiny and almost impalpable drop of their essence, the vast structure of recollection' (*ISLT* I: 54).

Although the taste of the madeleine evokes the memory of the past, this does not spontaneously emerge. Proust emphasizes the prolonged struggle to locate the past experience, in which voluntary and involuntary modes of remembering alternate. His initial 'exquisite pleasure' on tasting the tea leads him to drink a second mouthful, but this merely weakens its mnemonic efficacy: 'the potion is losing its virtue' (*ISLT* I: 51, 52). He attempts to deliberately call to mind the association that eludes him, but without success; and then, emptying his mind of everything except the taste of the tea, he finally feels something 'mounting slowly' within him. Although, finally, the memory 'sprang into being' (*ISLT* I: 53, 55), this is not the spontaneity of Bergson's pure memory but a much more laboured and prolonged process of recovery. In trying to locate his original experience, the narrator asserts that 'the truth I am seeking lies not in the cup but in myself' (*ISLT* I: 52); elsewhere, however, he suggests that the past is invested in external objects and places, so that his version of remembering comes to resemble, as Beckett has described it, 'a process ... of intellectualised animism' (1931: 23). The narrator describes his own affinity with 'the Celtic belief that the souls of those whom we have lost are held captive in some inferior being, in an animal, in a plant, in some inanimate object'. If we subsequently 'pass by the tree or ... obtain possession of the object', the souls become animate; 'they start and tremble, they call us by our name, and as soon as we have recognised them the spell is broken'. Our own past, Proust explains, is similarly hidden in some material object and can be unlocked by the sensation which that object gives us. Strikingly, however, it is for Proust entirely a matter of 'chance' as to whether we encounter this object within our lifetime (*ISLT* I: 51); he thus privileges in his account of memory the role of the accidental or the inadvertent.

The animistic quality of Proust's involuntary memory calls to mind the techniques of classical mnemonics; there, too, memory was located in a material object, albeit one that was located in the mind, and was reawakened when the rememberer 'passed by' the object in moving through the memorized location in which it was situated. As I argued in Chapter 1, however, the classical 'art of memory' elaborated a complex system of remembering, which aimed precisely to minimize the effects of chance; the object was carefully positioned so that it would be encountered once more and the associated memory revived. The classical mnemonic was also strongly reliant on a visual element: it utilized memory images that were as vivid and as striking as possible. Proust, in contrast, relegates the visual to a subsidiary role and privileges, instead, the physical senses of taste and smell. He makes clear that the sight of the madeleine alone had done nothing to restore the past to him, perhaps because it had become habitual to him from often seeing these pastries in bakers' shops, so that they ceased to be connected exclusively with Combray. Moreover, he indicates, in marked contrast to classical mnemonics, that the visual is more liable than the other senses to be buried or overlaid; it is, for him, an unreliable guardian of the past and it is accordingly not used as a catalyst for involuntary recollection in any of his most important memory sequences.

Proust frames his eight-volume *In Search of Lost Time* with two key sequences outlining involuntary memory. The 'madeleine' episode in *Swann's Way* is paralleled by a closing sequence in *Time Regained*, in which a flood of involuntary memories overwhelm the narrator and provide the novel's culmination as well as its justification, for it is this experience that determines the narrator to become a writer. The final sequence takes place after the narrator's confinement in a mental institution, brought on, we are led to believe, by the catastrophic effects of the First World War. Returning to Paris, he attends a reception at the Prince and Princess de Guermantes' and it is on his arrival, as he steps out of his carriage, that the uneven cobblestones of the courtyard provoke the first of his recollections. As in the 'madeleine' episode, involuntary remembering is preceded by a deliberate attempt at recollection: the narrator had sought in vain the day before to recall Venice, but his memories had remained 'as boring as an exhibition of photographs' (*ISLT* VI: 215). Losing his balance momentarily on the cobbles, however, recalls vividly to him 'the sensation which I had once experienced as I stood on two uneven stones in the baptistery of St. Mark's'; again, there is a lengthy struggle to locate the memory that has been evoked, and again Proust emphasizes the 'chance happening' that has caused the past to emerge (*ISLT*

VI: 218). In the following pages, as he waits alone in the library of the Guermantes' mansion for the music to finish, a flood of further memories washes over him, each evoked by a different physical stimulus: as a servant strikes a spoon against a plate, as he wipes his mouth on a napkin, and as the water cries in the pipes, the library successively gives way to a forest, the tide breaking on the shore at Balbec, and the cavernous dining room of the Grand Hotel in Balbec. The narrator is left with the exhilarating sensation that he has been 'freed from the order of time', and he even comes to doubt the very 'reality' and 'existence' of the self (*ISLT* VI: 225).

Upon leaving the library the narrator is, however, confronted by a cruel reminder of time, as he perceives the frailty and mortality that is now etched in the faces of those whom he knew in his youth. The focus of his attention quickly narrows to the figure of Mademoiselle de Saint-Loup; in her Swann–Guermantes parentage, the two 'ways' of his life converge, and he is accordingly able to recognize in her not only all of his former friends, but also himself. This leads him to reflect on the seemingly miraculous interconnectedness of life itself, so that the principle of chance seems to give way here to an alternative emphasis on the importance of fate:

> [T]he truth is that life is perpetually weaving fresh threads which link one individual and one event to another, and that these threads are crossed and recrossed, doubled and redoubled to thicken the web, so that between any slightest point of our past and all the others a rich network of memories gives us an almost infinite variety of communicating paths to choose from.
>
> (Proust *ISLT* VI: 428)

As Roger Shattuck has observed, the final sequence of memory instates a 'close, almost symmetrical relation of beginning and end' in the novel, while the appearance of Mademoiselle de Saint-Loup becomes 'the living symbol of the overall narrative movement towards reconciliation' (2001: 82). This interpretation notably accords closely with Proust's own insistence on memory as a gathering and unification, and on the particular joy that recollection can bring. However, Michael Sheringham rightly cautions us against placing too much emphasis, in reading *In Search of Lost Time*, on Proust's own declarations in relation to memory. Such a tendency can be discerned in Shattuck's reading, but Sheringham identifies it particularly with Mary Warnock's close emulation of Proust's emphasis on the 'pleasures' of remembering (1993: 291). Is Proustian memory, Sheringham enquires, as 'pleasurable' as Warnock (and, indeed, the narrator himself) seem to imply? For Sheringham, the answer is clearly no: 'memory in Proust', he contends, 'is by no means a purely joyous affair'. On the contrary, it is predicated on struggle and has as much power to 'disrupt and problematize identity' as to affirm it. Sheringham accordingly calls for an 'alternative anatomy' of memory in Proust, which brings out its darker and more foreboding aspects (1993: 292); in what follows, then, I would like to briefly sketch out one possible form that such an 'anatomy' might take.

The questions raised by Sheringham above are closely reflected by Terdiman, who regards Proustian involuntary memory as a 'utopian projection' and therefore seeks out 'the other side of involuntary memory's "joy"', its 'inevitable dystopian double' (1993: 237–8). He argues that, although Proust speaks of joy, his extended descriptions of involuntary memory paradoxically provide a distinctly contrary impression:

> In Proust these moments ... unstring subjectivity. They subvert consciousness and confront us with the incomprehensible; they produce a feeling of inexplicable and irresistible surrender, of a fantastic penetration by the irrational. There is something terrifying about experiences of this power.
>
> (Terdiman 1993: 212)

Proust's evocations of involuntary memory thus frequently recall moments of 'pain, suffering, or anguish' (Terdiman 1993: 217). The memories recovered are often of unhappiness and irreversible loss, so that they resuscitate or reactivate a former grief or sorrow. In this sense, then, involuntary memory bears a much closer resemblance to Freudian trauma than might be apparent from Proust's consistently celebratory account. Terdiman accordingly

contends that '[d]espite Proust's effort to mould our understanding of it in salvationist directions, the phenomenon Proust
narrates as involuntary memory uncannily recalls the description
in Freud of the pathologies of traumatic injury and involuntary
neurotic reminiscence' (1993: 200).

Turning to the most famous instance of involuntary memory,
the resurrection of Combray, Terdiman notes that its usual association with the 'madeleine' is mistaken on two counts: first, the
madeleine sequence represents the *second* evocation of Combray in
Swann's Way; and second, Combray is resurrected a final time in
the closing sequence of *Time Regained*. The first evocation of
Combray ('Combray I') follows on directly from Proust's opening
description of awakening. Here, the narrator recalls the prolonged
'anguish' that he suffered as a child on the nights when Monsieur
Swann came to visit, for he was sent to bed without a goodnight
kiss from his mother. This enforced separation from his mother
both prefigures and sets the pattern for the torments of his subsequent relationships with women, for he experiences for the first
time 'the anguish that comes from knowing that the creature one
adores is in some place of enjoyment where one is not and cannot
follow' (*ISLT* I: 34). The sequence concludes with the narrator's
observation that his memory is confined to those places that are
most closely associated with this affective drama: the hallway, the
staircase, and his bedroom in the house at Combray. The madeleine
episode ('Combray II') immediately intervenes, and the two contrasting memories seem, as Terdiman observes, to affirm Proust's
'glorification of the involuntary recapture of the past' (1993: 225).
The pain of the bedtime parting is therefore marginalized by
Proust's privileging of the second moment in the pairing, the full
recovery of the village in the madeleine incident. The positive
trajectory that is thereby established in *Swann's Way* is complicated,
however, by the final resurrection of Combray ('Combray III'),
which concludes the flood of involuntary memories that successively
overwhelm the narrator in the library of the Guermantes' palace.
Alighting unexpectedly upon George Sand's *François le Champi*,
the narrator recalls his mother reading the novel to him at bedtime when he was a child. This reawakening of the memory of
Combray represents for Terdiman a 'final evocation of anguish'

(1993: 234), for it returns the narrator to the pain of the bedtime drama. This is clearly signalled by Proust's invocation, in his description of the memory, of the figure of the split self, which he deploys throughout *In Search of Lost Time* at moments of acute pain or crisis. The narrator therefore does not initially recognize his childhood self, who suddenly and unexpectedly appears before him:

> This was a deeply buried impression that I had just encountered, one in which memories of childhood and family were tenderly inter-mingled and which I had not immediately recognised. My first reaction had been to ask myself, angrily, who this stranger was who was coming to trouble me. The stranger was none other than myself, the child I had been at that time, brought to life within me by the book, which knowing nothing of me except this child had instantly summoned him to its presence, wanting to be seen only by his eyes, to be loved only by his heart, to speak only to him.
>
> (Proust *ISLT* VI: 240)

The fracture of personality described here signals the intensity of affect which accompanies the memory, but also the presence of suffering. Its appearance at the end of the novel, although complicated by the unsettled state of Proust's manuscript at the time of his death, works against the celebratory account of memory established in *Swann's Way* and suggests, to Terdiman at least, that there is an 'archetypal experience of *pain*' in Proust. This, he argues, is elaborated through the reiterated memory of Combray, and provides 'a logic even more powerful than the metaphysics of [involuntary memory]'; a metaphysics which, viewed in this light, seems to act as a screen or defence against the pain of involuntary remembering, and to 'purposefully forge[t]' its more negative aspects (1993: 234; original emphasis). As Terdiman suggests, reading Proust against the grain of his own declarations reveals that his writing acts in powerful convergence with the tradition of the 'memory crisis'. Proust's descriptions of involuntary memory thus indicate the power of past suffering to overwhelm and, at times, incapacitate the present. In this light, Proust's celebratory accounts of memory can be read, in opposition to their stated meaning, as a defensive response to the anxieties of the 'memory crisis'; a response which, Terdiman concludes, 'rather than resolving [these anxieties]', paradoxically 'only calls them back more exactingly' (1993: 238). In the following section, I will move on to consider Proust's involuntary neurotic remembrances in the context of recent work on trauma and suggest that, although Proust's writing is necessarily very distinct from late-twentieth-century representations of traumatic experience, his work nevertheless has much to tell us of the haunting and pervasive power of the past.

TRAUMATIC MEMORIES

In the previous sections of this chapter, I have identified a persistent engagement with the notion of traumatic memory running through writers of the late nineteenth and early twentieth centuries. I have associated this preoccupation with Terdiman's analysis of a 'memory crisis', which manifested itself in a prevailing sense that there was both too little memory and too much, and suggested that the late twentieth century, in turn, witnessed a deepening or intensification of these concerns. In this section, I aim to outline the main areas of contestation in relation to the late-twentieth-century interest in trauma. My intention in so doing is to indicate that the key points of contemporary dispute originate in and refer back to debates that arose earlier in the century, and thereby trace a continuity of thinking about traumatic memory across the 'late-modern' period. Late-twentieth-century interest in trauma can, then, usefully be dated to 1980, when the American Psychiatric Association introduced into its *Diagnostic and Statistical Manual* the category of Post-Traumatic Stress Disorder (PTSD). This classification, which arose in the wake of the Vietnam War under increasing political pressure from returning veterans and clinical psychologists, gave official recognition for the first time to the symptoms of traumatic neurosis. As Cathy Caruth has noted, the official acknowledgement of the pathology provided a new diagnostic and analytical tool that was so powerful that it 'seemed to engulf everything around it: suddenly responses not only to combat and to natural catastrophes but also to rape, child abuse, and a number of other violent occurrences [were] understood in terms of PTSD' (1995a: 3). Controversy quickly arose, however, around the new categorization of trauma, most strikingly in relation to the phenomenon of dissociation.

Dissociative disorders were emphasized by the American Psychiatric Association in their diagnostic category of PTSD, especially in the 1994 revised edition of the *Diagnostic and Statistical Manual*. As noted by Ruth Leys (2000: 266), Cathy Caruth's influential definition of trauma in *Trauma: Explorations in Memory* seems to be influenced, in turn, by the model of dissociation. Caruth thus describes trauma as:

> a response, sometimes delayed, to an overwhelming event or events, which takes the form of repeated, intrusive hallucinations, dreams, thoughts or behaviors stemming from the event, along with numbing that may have begun during or after the experience, and possibly also increased arousal to (or avoidance of) stimuli recalling the event.
>
> (Caruth 1995a: 4)

Caruth's emphasis on the structure of the experience or, more precisely, its reception, so that the event is not assimilated fully at the time but only belatedly, and her interest in the ways in which trauma returns in the form of precise and literal nightmares, flashbacks and other re-enactments, are suggestive of dissociation. However, the most explicit description of trauma as dissociation in Caruth's edited volume is in the essay entitled 'The Intrusive Past', co-written by Bessel van der Kolk and Onno van der Hart. These neurobiologists argue that trauma is registered and encoded in the brain in a different way from ordinary memory. They place particular stress on the function of the hippocampus, which 'allows memories to be placed in their proper context in time and place'. In traumatic situations, they argue, the working of this part of the brain is suppressed, which 'results in amnesia for the specifics of traumatic experiences but not the feelings associated with them' (1995: 172). The 'memory' of trauma is thus not subject to the usual narrative or verbal mechanisms of recall, but is instead organized as bodily sensations, behavioural re-enactments, nightmares, and flashbacks. Although van der Kolk and van der Hart are keen to emphasize their distance from Freudian psychoanalysis, their work notably raises problems that call to mind my earlier discussion of Freud; namely, that the non-verbal registration of memory means that it is 'fixed in the mind and [is] not altered by the passage of time, or the intervention of subsequent experience' (1995: 172). The permanence of the memory trace that characterized the Freudian unconscious therefore continues to trouble contemporary trauma theory. Caruth refers to the belief of the neurobiologists that traumatic memory is 'engrav[ed]' on the mind or 'etch[ed] into the brain' (1995b: 153). Her language not only recalls Freud's metaphor of the wax tablet, but also clearly signals that problems of memory and inscription remain unresolved sites of contention in late-twentieth-century trauma theory. There is, then, a continuum of anxiety around these issues at the heart of the late-modern 'memory crisis', which is apparent both in the theorization of how trauma is registered or 'experienced' and, as I will go on to discuss, in the conceptualization – indeed, the very possibility – of the traumatic 'cure'.

The second key point of contention in contemporary trauma theory concerns whether trauma can be narrated or represented. This issue also intimately concerns the possibility of a 'cure', because narrative is seen as essential to cure in the context of PTSD. Van der Kolk and van der Hart emphasize that the integration of the traumatic memory into normal consciousness necessarily entails that it becomes subject to a 'narrative' memory system. 'By imagining ... alternative scenarios', they observe, 'many patients are able to soften the intrusive power of the original, unmitigated horror' (1995: 178). Nonetheless, they go on to express concern that, as a construction of the past, narrative memory distorts truth and becomes 'a sacrilege of the traumatic experience' (1995: 179). Caruth, too, articulates concerns that the traumatic 'cure' implies a dilution of the experience into the reassuring terms of therapy. Although the transformation of the trauma into narrative allows it to be verbalized and communicated, both to oneself and to others, Caruth attributes the reluctance of many survivors of trauma to tell a comprehensible story of the past to concerns regarding 'the loss ... of the event's essential incomprehensibility, the force of its *affront to understanding*' (1995b: 154; original emphasis). There is, then, a distinct tendency in recent theorizations of trauma towards an anti-therapeutic stance, a scepticism regarding the inherent value of telling one's story. Caruth accordingly calls for a mode of representing trauma that is able to transmit the gap or break in meaning that constitutes traumatic experience. Her point is an important one: she alerts us to the dangers of overly harmonizing the disruptions of trauma, so that the traumatic experience is covered over or repressed once more. Against this, however, Dominick LaCapra suggests that a mode of representation that too closely emulates its object risks 'acting (or playing) ... out' trauma, and potentially inhibits 'more critical analysis' (2001: 186). Again, these debates are suggestive of the unresolved ambiguities in Freudian psychoanalysis, discussed earlier in this chapter, concerning the purpose and efficacy of the 'talking cure'.

I would like to turn, in conclusion, to Charlotte Delbo's influential description of traumatic memory in her last work, *Days and Memory*. Delbo was a Holocaust survivor, who was arrested as a political prisoner by the French police in March 1942, and deported to Auschwitz and then Ravensbrück. She was released near the end of the war to the Red Cross, who sent her to Sweden to recover from severe malnutrition and ill health. She opens her account of memory with an image of a snake shedding its skin, 'emerging from beneath it in a fresh, glistening one'. The image captures the gradual recovery of her physical health, so that she slowly sheds 'the leaden stare out of sunken eyes, the tottering gait, the frightened gestures'. Her words are reassuring in their suggestion that the camp can be discarded, however slowly, and that new life can return. Nevertheless, she quickly makes apparent that only the 'visible traces' of Auschwitz can be left behind. The body memory of habit can gradually transform itself by returning to 'the gestures [of] an earlier life: the using of a toothbrush, of toilet paper, of a handkerchief, of a knife and fork, eating food calmly' (1990: 1). The underlying memory of Auschwitz remains buried within, however, and cannot be removed. Delbo thus initially conforms to the conventional narrative expectation that the past can be left behind, only to subsequently overturn or confound it, deliberately challenging and disorienting the reader.

Delbo's description of her underlying memory of Auschwitz emphasizes a split between intellectual and emotional memory. Elaborating further the imagery of the snake shedding its skin, she argues that the skin of memory paradoxically 'does not renew itself'; rather, it hardens into an 'impermeable' envelope, somewhat reminiscent of the 'baked' crust of the system *Cs*. in Freud's 'Beyond the Pleasure Principle', which contains the memory of Auschwitz and 'isolates it from my present self' (1990: 2). If Freud's protective layer was designed to protect from harmful *external* stimuli, however, Delbo's 'skin' emerges after the trauma and in response to it, and aims to isolate powerful and destructive *internal* energies. Delbo terms her underlying memory 'deep memory', and explains that it is particularly bound up with the senses; it 'preserves sensations, physical imprints'. Most of the time it is contained by the 'skin' that surrounds it, but Delbo describes her incessant fear that this skin will crack and the past overtake her once more. At times, the skin does indeed give way. This is particularly the case in dreams, when the past is relived with an overwhelming intensity and immediacy: 'the suffering I feel is so unbearable, so identical to the pain endured there, that I feel it physically, feel it throughout my whole body which becomes a mass of suffering' (1990: 3). In contrast to 'deep memory', Delbo also describes a memory of Auschwitz that can be communicated to others and is verbal rather than physical in nature. She terms this 'external memory' or 'intellectual memory', for it is connected with 'thinking processes' (1990: 3). It exists entirely separately from her deep memory of the event, and Delbo makes clear that she developed the mechanism of splitting after her release from the camps in order to be able to survive. This is a precarious strategy, however; existing within a 'twofold being' (1990: 3), she is unable to put the memory of the camps behind her or to relegate it safely to the past, and she accordingly does not live after Auschwitz but more precisely 'next to it' (1990: 2).

In 'The Intrusive Past', van der Kolk and van der Hart cite Delbo's description of her double existence as an example of clinical dissociation. Delbo remains, they argue, '(partially) aware' of her traumatic memories and is therefore able to tell the story of her traumatization with 'a mixture of past and present' (1995:

178). While this description is, as Victoria Stewart points out, in many ways 'an accurate characterization of Delbo's writing', it nevertheless fails to attend to the ways in which her text antici- pates their reading, advancing the dissociative model as a power- ful descriptive device rather than as a symptom to be diagnosed. Moreover, Stewart argues, Delbo evokes not the 'ossification' of the past, which would typify the clinical condition of dissociated memory, but rather a continually 'changing relationship' to her Auschwitz self (2003: 118). The model of dissociation thus acts in Delbo's writing both to convey the complexities and uncer- tainties of traumatic memory, and to assert survival as a constant and ongoing struggle to keep the past at bay.

Delbo's *Days and Memory* (*Le Mémoire et les jours*) deliberately echoes the title of Proust's early collection of stories, essays, and miscellaneous pieces, *Pleasures and Days* (*Les Plaisirs et les jours*), which was originally published in 1896. Delbo's pairing of deep memory and intellectual memory is itself suggestive of Proust's coupling of involuntary memory with voluntary memory. Like involuntary memory, deep memory is inextricably tied to the senses and it floods over the individual without any effort or control on her part. Intellectual memory recalls Proust's voluntary memory, because it offers up a past which remains essentially dead, lacking in potency and vivacity. Brett Ashley Kaplan has observed that Delbo's substitution of 'memory' for 'pleasure' in her title 'comments both on the similarity and the distance between these two terms' (2001: 326). For both writers, Kaplan argues, there is a certain pleasure in the process of remembering, which stems from 'the structure of the release of time'. Delbo is, like Proust, attentive to the suspended time of remembrance, and heightens or intensifies her meaning in 'deep memory' passages through highly sensual imagery. The crucial difference between the two writers, for Kaplan, lies in the content of the memories them- selves. If Proustian memory involves 'a pleasurable recreation of the past', Delbo points to 'the unimaginable pain of remember- ing' when the past concerns Auschwitz (2001: 328). Under the fear of re-entering this past, Delbo reverses Proustian memory, valuing intellectual memory over deep memory precisely because it can (usually) contain its horrors. Kaplan therefore highlights

Delbo's distance from Proust, her rewriting of the pleasure of remembrance as overwhelming pain. Following Terdiman, however, I argued earlier in this chapter that Proust's descriptions of involuntary memory often invoked intense pain, which was further heightened by the motif of the split self. Like Delbo's deep memory, Proust's involuntary memory is thus expressive of a past crisis. Read in this light, then, Delbo's title could be seen to signal continuity with Proust's concerns, and to register that Proustian involuntary memory, although concerned with very different experiences, nevertheless conveys something of the force of her own remembrances.

Delbo's affinity with Proust is further underlined in her discussion of thirst, which recalls the sipping of the tea that resurrects Combray. Again, Brett Ashley Kaplan stresses the distance that separates Delbo from Proust, noting that Delbo uses the word 'thirst' to refer not only to the everyday desire for a cup of tea, but also to the 'deep memory' thirst of Auschwitz that tormented her in the camp. In using the particular example of thirst, Delbo, he argues, 'was thinking of – and contradicting – Proust's claim that sense memories can be contained within cups of tea' (2001: 325). Again, however, an alternative reading is possible. For Proust, too, language contained two levels, so that the 'Combray' evoked by voluntary memory was not the same 'Combray' as the one that flooded his senses once he had tasted the madeleine dipped in tea. The fracturing of language registered by Delbo can, then, be read as a continuation and intensification of what was already implicit within Proust. Delbo therefore suggests her affinities with Proustian memory, which may not specifically address the problem of how to represent the worst, but does nevertheless illuminate the ways in which the least significant sensations, moments, or details can contain whole pasts. In this sense, Proust goes at least some of the way towards describing the involuntary nature of much traumatic remembering, particularly if we take into account Terdiman's perceptive analysis of the intense and unresolved pain involved in Proust's resurrection of Combray.

I have discussed Delbo's writing primarily in relation to the exigencies of memory, but she is also intimately concerned with the problem of forgetting. Although she unambiguously states that she 'cannot forget one moment' of her time in Auschwitz, Delbo articulates a powerful sense of the inextricability of remembering and forgetting, so that she is constantly caught between her desire to commemorate the dead, to hold them in her mind, and her equally urgent need to forget in order to live in the present. Delbo's concern with how it is possible to bear the intolerable burden of the past returns us to my discussion of Nietzsche at the opening of this chapter. I would like to conclude this chapter, therefore, by revisiting my earlier suggestion that Nietszche's case for oblivion in 'On the Uses and Disadvantages of History for Life' may no longer be appropriate given the moral and ethical burdens of remembrance in the late twentieth century. In order to address these concerns, I propose to briefly discuss Marc Augé's provocative essay *Oblivion*, and in particular his concluding section, 'A Duty to Forget'.

For Augé, there is an inextricable relation between remembering and forgetting. Oblivion throws our memories into relief and gives them shape and definition. Forgetting is an active agent in the formation of memories, and it is because memory and oblivion stand together, are entirely 'complicit' with one another, that both are necessary to enable life. The title of the final section of his essay calls to mind Nietzsche's admonition that there is a right time to forget as well as a right time to remember. Importantly, Augé includes in his discussion survivors of the concentration camps. They, he argues, 'do not need to be reminded of their duty to remember'; on the contrary, the past is ever present for them (2004: 87). Nevertheless, he contends that even survivors have a duty to forget: 'if they want to live again and not just survive, [they] must be able to do their share of forgetting … in order to find faith in the everyday again and mastery over their time'. Here, Augé echoes Delbo's sense of the fragile balance between survival and surviving the memory itself. His revival of Nietzsche emphasizes that none of us, perhaps especially the survivors themselves, can afford to 'forget to forget' (2004: 88). While I would agree with this in principle, I would also highlight Susan Suleiman's concern that Augé's insistence on forgetting 'seems somehow too easy'. As she notes, Augé does not specify exactly *how* forgetting can be achieved for Holocaust survivors; he moves too quickly over the persistence of memory's traces, which cannot easily be discarded. Although forgetting may indeed be desirable, to some degree, for the survivors of horrific crimes, Suleiman reminds us that they may also 'encounter some difficulties in carrying out such a program, especially when millions of other victims were also involved' (2006: 216).

Throughout this chapter, I have been concerned to elaborate an ongoing late-modern 'crisis' of memory, which places particular emphasis on the sense that there is too much memory. It therefore seems appropriate to close with a preliminary consideration of whether this is, indeed, the time to address in earnest the question of forgetting which was posed by Nietzsche. Certainly, forgetting seems important to survival itself and can, in addition, work against the solidification of narratives into too static or monumentalized a form. At the same time, however, forgetting cannot simply be prescribed in a manner that overlooks its difficulties, nor should the moral and ethical burdens of remembering be discounted. In the fourth and final chapter, I move on to address recent concerns over a perceived surplus or excess of remembering and commemoration in the context of contemporary 'collective memory' debates. I then conclude the volume by returning once again to the question of forgetting, and to the closely allied subject of forgiving, and by assessing in more detail both the claims and the perils of 'oblivion'.

4

COLLECTIVE MEMORY

In the last chapter, I argued that the late nineteenth and twentieth centuries have been pervaded by a sense that there is an excess of memory. I traced the development of the discourse of trauma, which is characterized by an emphasis on the overwhelming or possessive power of the past, from its nineteenth-century origins to the present. This final chapter aims to explore an alternative strand of twentieth-century memory discourse, namely the notion of 'collective memory'. 'Collective memory' emerged as an object of scholarly study in the early twentieth century. Maurice Halbwachs' two books *The Social Frameworks of Memory* (1925; translated as *On Collective Memory*, 1992) and *The Collective Memory* (published posthumously in 1950) argued that memory was a specifically social phenomenon. The first translation of Halbwachs' *The Collective Memory* into English in 1980 precipitated a scholarly boom. This was marked in particular by the publication of Yosef Hayim Yerushalmi's *Zakhor: Jewish History and Jewish Memory* (1982) and Pierre Nora's influential edited anthology *Les Lieux de mémoire* [Realms of Memory] (1984–92). Other key works followed in the early 1990s, including James Young's *The Texture of Memory* (1993) and Jay Winter's *Sites of Memory, Sites of Mourning* (1995).

The emergence of 'collective memory' in the twentieth century has often been seen, as Michael Rossington has pointed out, as 'a response to some influential late nineteenth- and early twentieth-century ... expositions of the nature of recollection', which regard it as 'a solitary act'. Romanticism, particularly the writing of William Wordsworth, associated memory with the idea of individual experience. This tendency, it has commonly been argued, was reinforced by the philosophy of Henri Bergson and the psychology of Sigmund Freud. Although such a reading is undoubtedly supported by Halbwachs' explicit refutation of Bergson's ideas, Rossington argues that it nevertheless risks ignoring the ways in which these earlier writers were also 'profoundly attentive ... to the behaviour and influence of groups' (2007b: 134). I would therefore suggest that it is more productive to see the recent preoccupation with 'collective memory' in dialogue with earlier traditions of thinking. The notion of a memory that is concerned not with individual experience, but with practices of remembrance that are defined and shaped by the surrounding culture, resonates with classical and early-modern conceptions of memory, which I discussed in Chapter 1. Charles Maier has proposed that the structures of rhetoric which were central to social and collective memory in these earlier periods were particularly 'cathected to and evoked by text'. For him, there has been a discursive shift, so that over time 'text has faded and landscape has intensified in its evocative capacity' (1993: 149). However, this misses the important role that was played by place in early-modern conceptions of memory, as outlined by Frances Yates. It is notable, then, that Pierre Nora explicitly cites Yates as his source for the phrase *lieux de mémoire*:

> Though not really a neologism, the term did not exist in French when I first used it ... I took it from ancient and medieval rhetoric as described by Frances Yates in her admirable book, *The Art of Memory* (1966), which recounts an important tradition of mnemonic techniques. The classical art of memory was based on a systematic inventory of *loci memoriae*, or 'memory places'.
>
> (Nora *RM* I: xv).

Nora seeks to revive and renew this 'classical art', providing in *Realms of Memory* an extensive, though far from exhaustive, inventory of the *loci memoriae* around which French collective memory is constructed. The emphasis on place in contemporary work on collective memory also recalls the central position that place occupied in Romantic memory; my reading of 'Tintern Abbey' at the close of Chapter 2 demonstrated that Wordsworth's recollections were triggered by place, and outlined the complex ways in which he used place to negotiate ideas of temporality, community, and the self. 'Collective memory' is also in close dialogue with the late-nineteenth-century thought which it seems explicitly to reject. Much attention has justifiably been paid to Halbwachs' contestation of Bergson's individualized psychology, but I argue below that Bergson's 'habit memory' also provides an essential element in the elaboration of collective memory, and helps to conceptualize its transmission. Although this aspect of Bergson's influence on collective memory has been less remarked upon, it is another indication that recent work on collective memory is inseparable from the long tradition of memory work that has formed the central focus of this study.

MAURICE HALBWACHS AND COLLECTIVE MEMORY

Although Maurice Halbwachs was born in Reims in 1877, his family moved to Paris when he was two years old. As a gifted scholar, he was enrolled at the prestigious Lycée Henri IV, and there he was taught by Henri Bergson, who was then at the beginning of his own career. Under Bergson's influence, Halbwachs determined to begin a career as a philosopher. Although he subsequently rejected Bergson's highly individualistic philosophy in favour of Emile Durkheim's emphasis on social psychology, Halbwachs' early encounter with Bergson left enduring traces in his work and thought. Before turning to Halbwachs' relation to Durkheim, I will consider Halbwachs' discussion of the individualistic philosophy, looking first at his approach to the unconscious and then at his analysis of dreams.

As I outlined in Chapter 3, Bergson believed that all of our past experiences are retained by memory; the events of our daily life are stored, complete and entire, in the unconscious and are available for future recollection. For Halbwachs, however, Bergson's model of 'ready-made images' stored in 'some subterranean gallery of our thought' (1980: 75) seems overly cumbersome, for it implies that we are perpetually burdened by the past: '[e]ach individual mind would in this manner drag behind itself the whole array of its memories' (1992: 39). His own model emphasizes the partial and incomplete nature of past recollections, and he attributes the ability to remember not to internal processes but to the reawakening of former experiences by external stimuli, such as meeting an old friend. Halbwachs considers that our world, even in childhood, is never a solitary one; from the earliest age, we carry with us and in us a number of distinct persons and are always enclosed within some group, be it familial, religious, political, economic, or social. In the course of our lives, we enter and form a part of a wide variety of groups. In belonging to a group we immerse ourselves in its milieu and identify with the thoughts and concerns that are common to it. The group, in Halbwachs' understanding, provides the individual with a 'framework' into which her remembrances are woven. Meeting an old friend acts as a stimulus to remembering because it reawakens the associations of the group to which we both belonged: meeting an old schoolfriend will therefore recall other former classmates, the classroom, the teachers, or our first day in a new school. Halbwachs makes clear that these memories are not stored inside of us: 'I do not mean that the remembrance or some part of it has to continue to exist as such in us' (1980: 25). Rather, what we have preserved and can retrieve is a schema, which comprises incomplete, wavering, and imprecise impressions that can then be fitted together under suitable stimuli. As Mary Douglas observes, remembering is, for Halbwachs, based on 'small, scattered and indistinct bits of the past' (1980: 5) and it is an activity of reconstruction in the present rather than the resurrection of the past.

For Bergson, pure memory, or the survival of personal memories in the unconscious, manifests itself particularly in dreams. Dreams represent our point of contact with the spontaneity and timelessness of the unconscious. Halbwachs subjects Bergson's understanding of dreams to close scrutiny in the opening sections of *On Collective Memory*. He initially seems to concur with Bergson in locating in dreams the spontaneity and the freedom that Bergson so admired. However, Halbwachs quickly goes on to qualify his description of the dream: it is not, for him, allied to memory because it lacks the organization, structure, continuity, and regularity that memory can provide. 'No real and complete memory ever appears in our dreams', Halbwachs explains, because they are 'composed of fragments of memory too mutilated and mixed up with others to allow us to recognize them' (1992: 41). Halbwachs contends that the dream differs from memory because it is the one area of human experience which is not rooted in a social context or structure: 'If purely individual psychology looks for an area where consciousness is isolated and turned in upon itself, it is in nocturnal life, and only there, that it will most be found' (1992: 42). Because dreams are not, like waking existence, firmly anchored in the system of social representations and structured by the social schema and frameworks of memory, they are rendered chaotic. In a comprehensive refutation of Bergson's approach, Halbwachs thus points out that dreams are not the privileged vehicle of pure memory that his mentor assumed: 'Far from being enlarged, free of the limitations of waking life, and far from gaining in extensiveness what it loses in coherence and precision, consciousness appears severely reduced and in a shrunken state in nocturnal life' (1992: 42). Dreams, then, may evoke images that have the appearance of memories, but Halbwachs is insistent that this is an illusion: 'The fact is that we are incapable of reliving our past while we dream' (1992: 41). Halbwachs' detachment of the dream from memory clearly separates him from Bergson's belief that the two are intimately connected. His analysis also demonstrates that, in the absence of the frames of collective memory, reasoning as such does not occur: 'individual memory' thus represents for Halbwachs a paradoxical formulation, because memory itself collapses once we enter into a state of isolation.

Halbwachs' shift from Bergson's influence to Durkheim's was the result of a period of study in Germany. On his return to Paris, he consulted Durkheim for advice on how to switch from philosophy to sociology. As Douglas remarks, this was a provocative gesture on Halbwachs' part: 'Halbwachs was ... not leaving Bergson's territory in any neutral sense, but rather was moving into a good position from which to prepare an attack on it' (1980: 6). Central to Durkheim's work was the project of understanding how social factors sustained and affected the individual consciousness. Of particular interest to him therefore were questions of religion, which represented, Douglas explains, a manifestation of 'the individual's experience of society as a moral force greater than himself, and requiring his allegiance' (1980: 8). Among Durkheim's most important achievements was his description of the periodic erup-tion of times of religious and cultural effervescence, which are characterized by ceremonies involving prolonged social interac-tion. For Durkheim, these were periods of pronounced cultural creativity; contrary to prevailing ideas, he therefore located crea-tivity not as an individual accomplishment, but rather as a col-lective phenomenon. As Douglas has pointed out, however, the problem with Durkheim's thought is that it only addresses peri-ods of exceptional cultural activity and therefore fails to account for what binds people together in more routine phases of social interaction. It is here, then, that Halbwachs' theory of collective memory makes a particular contribution, for it demonstrates the ways in which periods of apparent inactivity are filled with a variety of ritual and ceremonial acts of commemoration that not only help the recall of particular events but also serve to hold the community together.

For Halbwachs, any given society is composed of a number of different groups. Each group, be it a social class, an association, a corporation, or a family, has its own distinctive memories, which its members have constructed, often over long periods of time. Social memory is constantly transformed along with the groups themselves. As individual members of a group, especially older ones, become isolated or die, their memories are gradually eroded. Alternatively, the interests of one or several members, a conflict-ing event, or external circumstances can impinge upon a group, causing it to give rise to another group with its own particular memory. In this way, Halbwachs observes, past events and people are forgotten not out of social '[i]ll will nor indifference' but rather because 'the groups keeping these remembrances fade away' (1980: 82). The group memory itself comprises a body of shared concerns and ideas. In the foreground are remembrances of events and experiences that are of concern to the greatest number of members, while those concerning very few members or individuals fade into the background. Although it reflects and is refracted through the lives and personalities of individual group members, the collective memory represents the group's most stable and permanent element, and is sufficiently general and impersonal to retain its meaning when individual members drop out of the group and are replaced. Perhaps surprisingly, then, Halbwachs unequivocally asserts in *The Collective Memory* that 'it is individuals as group members who remember'. However, he immediately qualifies this position, observing that although individual members may 'vary in the intensity with which they experience [group memories]', the memories themselves are nevertheless 'common to all'. He then goes on to add that individual memory constitutes merely 'a viewpoint on the collective memory', a viewpoint that will change according to the individual's relationship with other groups (1980: 48). Individual memory is therefore effectively displaced by Halbwachs and absorbed into the collective memory.

A number of critics have responded to Halbwachs' emphasis on the collective memory, at the expense of individual acts of recollection. Noa Gedi and Yigal Elam have pointed out that, although Halbwachs' position may seem 'a natural derivative of the Durkheimian position', it is in effect 'quite a deviation from it'. In spite of Durkheim's emphasis on the social, they argue, he does not make any statement regarding individual representations, nor does he deny that they exist. Halbwachs thus goes beyond Durkheim, 'abandoning the fine distinction ... between individual and collective representations' (1996: 36). For Paul Ricoeur, too, Halbwachs' work on collective memory 'cross[es] an invisible line'. This line, Ricoeur goes on to explain, separates 'the thesis "no one ever remembers alone" from the thesis "we are not an authentic subject of the attribution of memories"' (2004: 122); again, then, the issue at stake here is Halbwachs' failure to recognize the individual. For Ricoeur, however, Halbwachs' 'surprising dogmatism' on this point does not provide grounds for dismissing his otherwise remarkable body of work. In the first instance, Ricoeur observes, 'it was in the personal act of recollection' that the mark of the social was initially sought by Halbwachs, and accordingly to retain a belief that the act of recollection remains personal to some degree cannot simply be 'denounced as a radical illusion'. He also points out that Halbwachs' argument can be read against his own intention. In this sense, Halbwachs' belief that the collective memory is inflected by the individual's relationship with different groups opens up the very possibility for individual agency, because it presupposes that the individual consciousness has 'the power to place itself within the viewpoint of the group and, in addition, to move from one group to another' (2004: 123).

Other critics have sought to respond to Halbwachs by providing a more nuanced terminology, which might enable a more precise conception of the relationship between individuals and collectives. Wulf Kansteiner has thus distinguished between 'collective memories' and 'collected memories'. 'Collective memories' closely correlate with Halbwachs' notion. They describe 'shared communications about the meaning of the past' that are 'anchored in the life-worlds of individuals who partake in the communal life of [a group]' (2002: 188). A 'collected memory', on the other hand, comprises 'an aggregate of individual memories which behaves and develops just like its individual composites' (2002: 186). In a similar vein, Avishai Margalit has suggested introducing a distinction between 'shared memory' and 'common memory'. 'Shared memory' closely approximates Halbwachs' collective memory. 'A shared memory', Margalit observes, 'integrates and calibrates the different perspectives of those who remember [an] episode ... into one version' (2002: 51–2). 'Common memory', however, more closely resembles Kansteiner's 'collected memory'; it 'aggregates the memories of all those people who remember a certain episode which each of them experienced individually' (2002: 51). In proposing an alternative form of social remembering to collective memory, Kansteiner and Margalit seek to relocate the individual within the collective, thereby emphasizing the role of human agency in the construction of shared or social memories.

Halbwachs most clearly signals his distinctive contribution to Durkheimian sociology in his discussion of the distinction between history and memory. For Halbwachs, collective memory can stretch back into the past a varying distance, but it is most preoccupied with events that are within living memory. Group memory thus typically extends back over a duration that does not exceed, and is usually much shorter than, the average span of a human life. Social groups have often therefore participated in the events with which they are concerned, and are capable of grasping them directly. History arises, Halbwachs argues, when the past 'is no longer included within the sphere of thought of existing groups' (1980: 106). It is only once social groups have disappeared and their thoughts and memories have vanished that history preserves and fixes the past. For Halbwachs, this introduces a crucial distinction between the image of the past that is produced by collective memory and that produced by history. Group memory is focused on its own relations and consequently feels that it has retained a constant identity over time. Because collective memory perpetuates the feelings and images that form the substance of the group's identity, it produces a sense of the past which is 'without rupture or upheaval' and in which 'nothing has radically changed' (1980: 85, 86). History, on the contrary, by focusing on the whole, tends to emphasize the alterity of the past and is persuaded that societies are in constant transformation. It accordingly produces 'a record of changes' and is 'not interested in ... intervals when nothing apparently happens, when life is content with repetition in a somewhat different, but essentially unaltered, form' (1980: 86, 85). It is, then, in his formulation of the distinction between history and collective memory that Halbwachs' main contribution to Durkheim's thought, namely to provide an account of how societies are bound together in phases of seeming routine or inaction, finds one of its clearest articulations.

A notable shortcoming of Halbwachs' distinction between history and memory has been identified by Jan Assmann. For Assmann, Halbwachs does not take systematic account of those collective memories which extend beyond the span or range of a lifetime. Once 'the contemporary reference [was] lost', he contends, 'Halbwachs ... stopped at this juncture' and too readily assumed that "[m]émoire" [was] transformed into "histoire" (1995: 128). Assmann thus seeks to distinguish more precisely between 'communicative memory' and 'cultural memory'. 'Communicative memory' approximates closely to Halbwachs' understanding of collective memory. It has a very limited temporal horizon, usually extending eighty to one hundred years at most, and it is based solely on everyday communications. It is thus, by definition, strongly influenced by contemporaries of the event in question. 'Cultural memory', in contrast, is primarily concerned with events from a more distant past, beyond living memory. The memory of events is retained either through cultural formation (texts, rites, or monuments) or through institutional commemoration (recitation, practice, observance). Cultural memory is particularly characterized by its distance from the everyday, or its transcendence. Often formalized through ceremony, cultural memory typically depends upon a specialized practice for its transmission, so that there are designated bearers of memory. Assmann's elaboration of 'cultural memory' thus seeks to develop Halbwachs' thinking by attending carefully to those collective memories which are concerned with a more distant past.

Assmann's writing is closely complemented by Paul Connerton's incisive study *How Societies Remember* (1989). Connerton's attention is also drawn to Halbwachs' failure to account for collective memories that extend beyond a single generation or lifetime. He thus critiques Halbwachs in the following terms:

> If we follow the thread of Halbwachs's argument we are inevitably led to the question: given that different groups have different memories which are particular to them, how are these collective memories passed on within the same social group from one generation to the next? Halbwachs does little more than hint at answers to this question.
>
> (Connerton 1989: 38)

In seeking to fill in the gap left by Halbwachs, Connerton argues persuasively for the importance of habit in the transmission of collective memory. In this context, then, the work of Bergson, and especially his concept of 'habit memory', becomes a suggestive point of departure for conceptualizing collective memory, and seems to be particularly well suited to bridging the methodological gap in relation to its inter-generational transmission. I argued in Chapter 3 that Bergson's habit memory recognized the important role of the body in modes of remembering. It described the ways in which memory accumulates in the body through certain forms of repetitive behaviour, so that the past comes to be relived or re-enacted in the present. In arguing for the importance of habit to social forms of remembering, Connerton accordingly seeks to emphasize the ways in which collective memory, too, is reliant on the body. For Assmann, the incorporated practices which could transmit cultural memory from one generation to the next comprised commemorative ceremonies and rituals. Connerton, too, sees these social practices as essential to the preservation of group memories. All rituals are characterized by the bodily performance of set postures, gestures, and movements, which are highly formalized, easily predictable, and readily repeatable. Their power arises from their habituation, so that they form an automatic sequence of movements that can readily identify those who are members of a particular group. Commemorative ceremonies are distinguishable from other rituals because they explicitly refer to prototypical persons or events, which are understood to have a historical or mythological existence. Rites of this sort accordingly possess a characteristic of ritual re-enactment, which is central to the shaping of collective memory. An image of the past is, then, not simply conveyed and sustained by ritual performances; it is also brought to life in the present and relived through direct embodiment and gestural repetition.

In addition to Assmann's emphasis on commemorative ceremonies, Connerton also identifies another form of incorporated remembering. The alternative incorporated practices with which he is concerned are characterized by a lesser degree of formality than the invariant rites of commemorative ceremonies. They consist instead in certain forms of bodily proprieties that distinguish particular social groups, and are remembered and reproduced as habitually observed rules of decorum. Such codes of bodily etiquette preserve and pass on the memory of certain values and behaviours that the group holds to be important. More than this, however, it is precisely because the gestures performed are movements to which the performers are entirely habituated that such practices act as a persuasive means of distinguishing those who belong to the group from those who do not. As Connerton points out, the narrator's description of his friend, the Marquis Robert de Saint-Loup, in Marcel Proust's *Within a Budding Grove*, provides a particularly compelling example of such an incorporated practice. Although Saint-Loup consciously wishes to disown the privileges and characteristics of an aristocrat, Proust demonstrates that he has so thoroughly incorporated the habits of the nobility that his every movement betrays his origins. The narrator thus observes:

> [T]here were moments when my mind distinguished in Saint-Loup a personality more generalised than his own, that of the 'nobleman', which like an indwelling spirit moved his limbs, ordered his gestures and his actions ... The discovery in him of this pre-existent, this immemorial being, this aristocrat who was precisely what Robert aspired not to be, gave me intense joy, but a joy of the mind rather than the feelings. In the moral and physical agility which gave so much grace to his kindnesses, in the ease with which he offered my grandmother his carriage and helped her into it, in the alacrity with which he sprang from the box when he was afraid that I might be cold, to spread his own cloak over my shoulders, I sensed ... above all the certainty or the illusion in the minds of [the] great lords of being 'better than other people', thanks to which they had not been able to hand down to Saint-Loup that anxiety to show that one is 'just as good as the next man', that dread of seeming too assiduous of which he was indeed wholly innocent and which mars with such stiffness and awkwardness the most sincere plebeian civility.
>
> (Proust *ISLT* II: 365–6)

The essential distinction that Proust is making here, then, is the difference between being able to recognize a mode of behaviour and being able to incorporate it. Saint-Loup betrays himself not only through his gestures and actions but through the very ease with which he performs them; his body, Connerton observes, 'is [that] of one who has the habit of ruling' (1989: 90). In identifying such incorporating practices, Connerton draws to our attention a particularly effective system of mnemonics through which socially encoded systems of behaviour are transmitted and preserved. His writing provides an alternative focus to Assmann's emphasis on commemorative ceremonies, and he demonstrates persuasively, through his discussion of the extent to which rules of conduct and etiquette become sedimented within the body, that Bergson's habit memory occupies an important, if hitherto neglected, place in the theorization of collective memory.

Halbwachs addresses the issue of incorporated social practices at most length in his discussion of religious collective memory. The memory of religious groups, he points out, 'claims to be fixed once and for all' (1992: 92). If the rest of social life develops over the passage of time, religion has an object which is eternal and immutable and its commemorative acts symbolize this eternity through their repetition and uniformity. Taking Christianity as his example, Halbwachs identifies 'rites' as encompassing 'a body of gestures, words, and liturgical objects established in a material form'. For Halbwachs, the rite notably forms 'the most stable element of religion' and this is precisely because of its incorporated elements: 'it is largely based on material operations which are constantly reproduced and which are assured uniformity in time and space by rituals and the priestly body' (1992: 116). Rites also derive their power and efficacy from their commemoration and re-enactment of a religious memory. For Christians, the Communion thus maintains and reproduces the remembrance of the Last Supper. Halbwachs therefore designates it as the object of religion to maintain the remembrance of the past over a long temporal period, and to prevent it from being corrupted by intervening memories or beliefs. Although religions seek to isolate themselves from other social groups, Halbwachs concludes that they nevertheless conform to the same laws as every other instance of collective memory: they do not preserve the past but 'reconstruct it with the aid of material traces, rites, texts, and traditions left behind by that past' (1992: 119).

If Halbwachs regards the preservation and transmission of memory as central to religious practice, Jan Assmann has astutely noted that such a formulation applies most sharply, not to Christianity, but to the Jewish religion. Strikingly, then, this is a subject which Halbwachs, an assimilated Jew, '[does] not treat and hardly even mentions' (1995: 129 n. 16). For discussion of the Jewish religion and collective memory, we must therefore turn instead to Yosef Yerushalmi. Yerushalmi identifies the Jews as the archetypal people of memory, who adopted history only recently and then only in part. History, he contends, 'is by no means the principal medium through which the collective memory of the Jewish people has been addressed or aroused' (1996: 5). Rather, the continuity of Jewish memory has been sustained through the channels of ritual and liturgy. The major festivals of the Jewish year thus remember the historical narrative of a community. Passover commemorates annually the exodus of the people from Egypt; Seder reminds practising Jews of the moment in which their community was freed from bondage; Purim recalls the events related in the Book of Esther; while Hanukkah celebrates the story of the purification of the Temple. These memories, reawakened through commemorative rituals, provide for the Jews a powerful sense of 'evocation and identification' (1996: 44). Although Yerushalmi risks too easy an opposition between history and memory, which positions memory as an anti-historical discourse, his writing is nevertheless suggestive in the context of Halbwachs' work on religion and collective memory, for he argues that com- memorative ceremonies assume a particular significance in keeping memories alive over many generations. Yerushalmi also indicates that the inscribed practices of historiography are less important than the incorporated practices of ritual and liturgy in passing down the remembrance of the most important events in the communal life of the Jewish people over successive gen- erations.

Halbwachs identifies one other incorporated practice that is essential to religious groups, namely their reliance on place. Religious remembrance is particularly evoked by holy sites and places, and specific locations and buildings are consecrated to religion or habitually occupied by religious communities. Halbwachs notes that place takes on a distinct role for religious groups, so that entering a religious building does not so much recall to us our relationships with the group that holds similar beliefs, as awaken in us the mental disposition which is conducive to worship, 'a certain uniform bent of thought and sensibility' (1980: 152). However, he also argues that place is of particular importance to religious groups because of their claim to be unchanging. Since they must persuade themselves that they remain the same, while everything else is in transformation around them, they rely on the stability and the sense of permanence that place can provide: 'the collective thought of the group of believers has the best chance of immobilizing itself and enduring when it concentrates on places' (1980: 156). Despite their claims to uniqueness, however, Halbwachs notes that religious groups once again conform to the same laws of collective memory as other social groups. Individuals situate their recollections within mental spaces provided by the group, but Halbwachs insists that these mental spaces always receive support from and refer back to material spaces. For the family group, the interior space of the home gives a sense of its own continuity over time. The physical objects of the home with which the group members are in daily contact change little or not at all, and so give the illusion of rediscovering the past in the present. The space of the city provides a sense of stability for urban groups. Indeed, the collective memory of city dwellers is affected far more by a disturbance in their physical surroundings, Halbwachs notes, than by the most violent national upheavals that leave the buildings intact: 'the inhabitants pay disproportionate attention to what I have called the material aspect of the city. The great majority may well be more sensitive to a certain street being torn up, or a certain building or home being razed, than to the gravest national, political, or religious events' (1980: 131). For Halbwachs, then, collective memory necessarily unfolds within a spatial framework, which allows social groups to 'enclose and retrieve [their] remembrances' (1980: 157). It also provides the sense of permanence or of not having changed through time that is such a central feature of Halbwachs' conception of collective remembrance.

Halbwachs' emphasis on the role of place in collective memory would perhaps lead us to expect that the nation would take on particular significance for him as a social grouping. Certainly for Pierre Nora the nation becomes the most important community of memory, as I will discuss in the next section. For Halbwachs, however, although he recognizes that the nation is a privileged locus of collective memory within modernity, there are many, more restricted groups between the individual and the nation, and it is these to which his attention is drawn. He thus argues that the frameworks of national memory do not 'represent the essence of what I call collective memory' (1980: 77). Although the life of the individual is encompassed within national life, the nation cannot be said to be interested in the lives of each of its members, as is possible within more intimate social groupings. It is for this reason that the lives of individuals are ordinarily limited in outlook to the smaller groups circumscribed by family, work, and local community. Halbwachs acknowledges that there are exceptional occasions of national importance that simultaneously alter the lives of all citizens, and these events, although rare, offer a temporal landmark around which other memories come retrospectively to be shaped. We could think, for example, of the assassination of John F. Kennedy, or the attack on the World Trade Center of 11 September 2001, as constituting such events in the American collective memory. Ordinarily, however, Halbwachs makes clear that the nation 'is too remote from the individual for him to consider the history of his country as anything else than a very large framework with which his own history makes contact at only a few points' (1980: 77).

Although Halbwachs has exerted a powerful influence on subsequent work, *The Collective Memory* was left unfinished at his death and was, in the words of Lewis A. Coser, 'akin to a skeleton' (1992: 2). Halbwachs' last years, as an assimilated Jew in occupied France, were marked by increasing tragedy. He suffered the family deaths of his brother-in-law, Dr Georges Basch, who committed suicide in 1940, and his father-in-law and mother-in-law, Victor Basch and his wife, who were both murdered under the Vichy regime. Outraged by the deaths of his parents-in-law, both eighty years old, Halbwachs went to Lyon to protest and to inquire about the circumstances. He was arrested on the spot and transported to Buchenwald concentration camp, where he died a few months before the liberation. In a moving epilogue to Halbwachs' death, Jorge Semprún, who was also imprisoned in Buchenwald and who had been taught by Halbwachs in Paris, provided an account of nursing Halbwachs through his final illness in his memoir *Literature or Life*. After his friend's death, which left Semprún overwhelmed with grief, it was his task, in the camp office at Buchenwald, to erase Halbwachs' name and number from the index card, so that a new inmate would be able to reuse the number and another name could be written on the card:

> I took out the index card with Maurice Halbwachs's name on it, and I erased that name: a living person would now be able to take the dead man's place. By a living person, I mean: a future corpse. I did every-thing necessary. I carefully erased his family name, Halbwachs, and his first name, Maurice – all signs of identity. I held the rectangular index card in the palm of my hand. It had become blank and white once more, ready for another life to be written on it, and a new death.
>
> (Semprún 1997: 43)

If Semprún's job within the camp was to erase all sign that Halbwachs had existed, his memoir seeks to reverse this process and to re-inscribe Halbwachs' name and memory. Against the logic of infinite substitution, which defines the camp prisoner even after he has died, Semprún asserts in his memoir the unique singular-ity of his friend and teacher, and he seeks to provide Halbwachs with a fitting memorial, transforming the blank, white surface of willed forgetting into the carefully traced and lovingly inscribed figures of his name: Halbwachs, Maurice.

PIERRE NORA AND THE 'SITES OF MEMORY'

In his highly acclaimed volume *The Vichy Syndrome*, Henry Rousso outlined a narrative of post-war French national memory (and forgetting) that has since been frequently cited and retold. According to Rousso, the renewal of left–right political divisions in France immediately after the war impeded the national work of mourning. The 1950s inaugurated a period of forgetting, in which the memories of the Occupation and of Vichy were 'repressed' in favour of myths that celebrated the heroism of the Resistance:

> From 1954 to 1971 the subject of Vichy became less controversial ... The French apparently had repressed memories of the civil war with the aid of what came to be a dominant myth: 'resistancialism' ... By

> resistancialism I mean, first, a process that sought to minimize the importance of the Vichy regime and its impact on French society, *including its most negative aspects*; second, the construction of an object of memory, the 'Resistance', whose significance transcended by far the sum of its active parts (the small groups of guerrilla partisans who did the actual fighting) ...; and, third, the identification of this 'Resistance' with the nation as a whole, a characteristic feature of the Gaullist myth.
>
> (Rousso 1991: 10; original emphasis)

There was, in these years, a failure to address the 'dark years' of the Vichy regime under German occupation (1940–44). The more shameful aspects of Vichy, and particularly the collaboration with the Germans in rounding up and deporting 75,000 Jews from French soil, became a taboo subject in French public discourse. From the early 1970s on, however, in what Rousso designates as a 'return of the repressed', Vichy returned to public consciousness (1991: 10). In particular, a series of highly publicized legal trials brought Vichy back to public attention, beginning with the 1987 trial of Klaus Barbie, a Nazi functionary notorious for his role in persecuting Jews in Lyon, and culminating with the trial of Maurice Papon in 1997, a highly placed French bureaucrat who had been in charge of the round-up of Jews in Bordeaux. Films also began to address these sensitive topics. Marcel Ophüls' *The Sorrow and the Pity* (1971) reminded the French about Vichy anti-Semitism and collaboration. Claude Lanzmann's *Shoah* (1985) also made a considerable impact on French audiences. Even if Lanzmann was almost exclusively concerned with the persecution of the Jews in eastern Europe, his film contributed to a growing awareness in France of Jewish suffering and the Holocaust. Although Rousso's use of psychoanalytic concepts to describe collective processes is undoubtedly problematic, his overall narrative is, as Nancy Wood has observed, 'illuminating' (1999: 222). His elaboration of a national identity crisis in France has resonances beyond Vichy, and calls to mind other topics that the French sought unsuccessfully to put behind them, in particular the 'dirty wars' in Indo-China and Algeria, and the torture that was practised by the French army in Algeria.

The crisis of French national identity outlined by Rousso formed an important background to Pierre Nora's ambitious historical project *Les Lieux de mémoire* (1984–92; translated into English as *Realms of Memory*, 1996–98). For Nora, the notion of a unitary national history had become problematic, if not impossible, in France due to the politicization of memory. His multi-volume edited project therefore sought a new way to articulate history, which focused less on specific events than on the ways in which they had been interpreted by, or divided into, competing spheres of political influence. Nora therefore used the notion of collective memory, as Lawrence D. Kritzman has pointed out, to trace 'the metamorphoses that French memory ha[d] undergone in recent times', its move away from the single, unitary framework of the nation to smaller configurations or identities. Although Nora therefore seems to echo Halbwachs' emphasis on more intimate memory communities, Kritzman argues that his focus remains firmly attached to the nation, so that 'the memorial process activates a renewed sense of national self-consciousness' (1996: xi). For Wood, too, Nora's relation to Halbwachs is more complex than it initially appears. Nora's work on French collective memory represents a 'radical reworking' of Halbwachs, and *Realms of Memory* comprises 'nothing less than a radical upheaval in the way the phenomenon of "collective memory" can henceforth be conceived' (1999: 17).

In 'Between Memory and History', his introduction to the first volume of *Realms of Memory*, Nora refers to Halbwachs in distinguishing between memory and history. Like Halbwachs, he defines memory as 'embodied in living societies', while history is 'the reconstruction … of what is no longer'. Nora also, following Halbwachs, contrasts memory as 'multiple' and 'plural' with the unitary nature of history (*RM* I: 3). Although he initially presents his project as closely tied to Halbwachs' work, Nora soon departs from his influence however. The introduction goes on to outline a history of memory in three distinct phases or periods: the 'pre-modern', which represented an era of natural, spontaneous, and unselfconscious memory practices; the 'modern', which coincided with the rise of the nation state and in which a historical consciousness began to prevail over a memorial one; and the current 'postmodern' age of media culture, in which representations of the past emerge and are consumed at the rapid and frantic pace of media consumption itself. The narrative of memory that Nora elaborates is implicitly one of decline and loss, in which there was a 'fall from grace' during the course of the nineteenth century, an expulsion from a realm of intuitive memory that cannot now be recovered. Kritzman rightly notes that, in tracing such a trajectory, Nora's project 'represents the symptomatology of a certain form of cultural melancholia' (1996: ix). His work is imbued with the sense that something essential has been lost from French national values and culture, something that is intimately associated for him with the disappearance of the peasantry and the rhythms of a rural life. Responding to the sense of national crisis outlined above, Nora thus risks retreating into a nostalgic idealization of the past, and creating too binary an opposition between a living memory tradition, which has now vanished, and the abstract rationalizations of history that remain.

Nora's distinction between memory and history is notably also a distinction between incorporation and inscription. In defining 'true memory', the unselfconscious memory practices and traditions that have largely been lost, Nora associates them particularly with the body; they comprise 'gestures and habits, unspoken craft traditions, intimate physical knowledge, ingrained reminiscences, and spontaneous reflexes'. In contrast, modern memory, transformed by its passage through history, is associated with writing. It is the memory of the 'archive', and relies on 'the visibility of the image' (*RM* I: 8). For Halbwachs, as I noted above, collective memory could be transmitted through either inscribed or incorporated practices; for Nora, however, there is a notable suspicion of writing, which is associated exclusively with memory that has been tainted by history. For Nora, inscription is necessary because memory is no longer experienced from within; it is therefore reliant upon an external prop or a tangible reminder. For this reason, the archive has become a contemporary obsession, which has proliferated beyond our control: 'we attempt to preserve not only all of the past but all of the present as well' (*RM* I: 8). Unable to determine what of the present might be worth preserving, we 'refrain from destroying anything and put everything in archives instead'. However, this indiscriminate practice leads not to improved remembering, but rather to a 'hypertrophy of memory' (*RM* I: 9). The argument that Nora advances here is familiar to us from Chapter 1; as Ricoeur notes, this is 'truly the tone of Plato's *Phaedrus*' (2004: 403). It is not simply that inscription acts for Nora as an external supplement and is an object of distrust. Additionally, Nora echoes Plato's accusation that writing represents a poison rather than a remedy. The archive is accordingly associated for Nora not with remembering but with forgetting: in depositing material in the archive, we are also 'delegating the responsibility for remembering', discarding our memories 'as the snake deposits its shed skin' (*RM* I: 8).

Nora's *lieux de mémoire*, or 'sites of memory', arise against the backdrop of the historical periods of memory that he has outlined. Not solely a matter of topographical places, although 'sites of memory' can certainly take this form, these represent, as Ricoeur explains, 'external marks, as in Plato's *Phaedrus*, from which social behaviors can draw support for their everyday transactions' (2004: 404). *Lieux de mémoire* are associated for Nora not with memory but with history; indeed, they exist only because there are no longer any *milieux de mémoire*, sites in which memory is a real part of everyday experience. *Lieux de mémoire* thus originate in the sense of rupture and loss that Nora views as constitutive of the modern; instead of dwelling among our memories, we now consecrate sites to them, displaying a deliberate will to remember. Lacking a sense of spontaneous memory, we 'create archives, mark anniversaries, organize celebrations, pronounce eulogies, and authenticate documents because such things no longer happen as a matter of course'. In his introductory essay, then, Nora clearly positions the *lieux de mémoire* as substitutes for an authentic and immediate collective memory; they represent 'the rituals of a ritual-less society; fleeting incursions of the sacred into a disenchanted world' (*RM* I: 7). Across the project as a whole, however, Nora displays a notable ambivalence in his approach, which complicates his opening argument, and threatens to undermine and undo the narrative of decline that he has so carefully established.

In the second instalment of *Les Lieux de mémoire*, which was entitled *La Nation* (1986), Nora charted the role played by memory in the construction of the French nation, and identified the key 'sites of memory' that provided a sense of social cohesion and identity. With the third and final instalment, *Les France* (1992), Nora seemed to shift his attention to the historical eclipse of France as a 'memory-nation'. He argued that over the last twenty years, France has witnessed the decline of national memories and a corresponding increase in 'patrimonial' sites of memory, more fragmented and partisan memory places which represent local rather than national loyalties and claims of allegiance. Patrimonial memory, Nora explained in his concluding essay, 'came from the grass roots, from the provinces' and it 'connoted anything that made people feel that they had roots in a particular place'. Embedded in the regional and the particular, this form of memory was particularly focused on traditions that had been passed down from generation to generation: 'It ... took up residence among forgotten customs and ancient techniques, good local wines, songs and dialects' (*RM* III: 625). However, although Nora seems to be focusing here on the increasing plurality and democratization of collective memory processes, it is notable that the nation remains the primary reference point for his work. Nostalgic for France's loss of a firm footing in the world, Nora's 'underlying aim', argues Perry Anderson, 'was the creation of a *union sucrée* in which the divisions and discords of French society would melt away in the fond rituals of postmodern remembrance' (2004: 10). Anderson's critique brings to light the extent to which Nora, in identifying those symbols and rituals that bind the nation together, has omitted from his study more uncomfortable aspects of the French national past. Perhaps unsurprisingly, therefore, Nora's project became co-opted by the very forces that it set out to study, becoming, even before it was completed, a scholarly *lieu de mémoire* in its own right. As Nora opines in his concluding essay: '[n]o sooner was the expression *lieu de mémoire* coined than what was forged as a tool for maintaining critical distance became the instrument of communication par excellence' (*RM* III: 609).

For Anderson, Nora's project may have been more instructive in producing a critical history of French collective memory if it had focused on areas of social conflict and division, and comprised not a catalogue of *lieux de mémoire* but of *lieux d'oubli*, 'sites of forgetting'. Certainly, as Anderson goes on to demonstrate, a survey of Nora's own 'sites of forgetting', the gaps and absences in his project, provides the basis for a focused and incisive critique of his work, and helps to identify the key areas that he has expressly avoided because of their potentially divisive effect. Tony Judt has drawn attention to the 'bizarre' absence from *Realms of Memory* of 'Napoleon Bonaparte or his nephew Louis Napoleon, or even ... the political tradition of *bonapartisme* that they bequeathed to the nation'. In seeking to account for this omission, Judt contends that, certainly in the case of Louis Napoleon, Nora's disinterest may reflect 'a broader lack of concern with towns, town planning and urbanism in general: a perhaps excessive care to record France's love affair with its peasants and its land' (1998: 54). For Anderson, however, the significance of Nora's neglect of Napoleon lies elsewhere; namely, in his concern to overlook 'the entire imperial history of the country, from the Napoleonic conquests, through the plunder of Algeria under the July Monarchy, to the seizure of Indochina in the Second Empire and the vast African booty of the Third Republic'. Anderson regards Nora's silence on this issue not only as surprising in the context of his courageous critique of the Algerian war in his youth, but also as a significant failing of the project: 'What are the *lieux de mémoire* that fail to include Dien Bien Phu?' (2004: 10). In addition to Nora's silence on imperial history, Judt also draws attention to his consistent tendency to treat Catholic Christianity 'as the essence of true Frenchness'. Nora's overemphasis on Catholicism results in a relative neglect of French Protestant history, so that, as Judt remarks, '[t]here is no entry in these pages for the massacre of Protestants on St Bartholomew's Day, 1572 – a French "memory date" if ever there was one' (1998: 56). This silence is particularly striking, as Anderson observes, when set against the remarks of the historian Ernest Renan, writing at the end of the nineteenth century, who pointed out that a nation is defined as much by what it has forgotten as by what it chooses to remember. Renan's example of national forgetting was precisely the French slaughter of the Protestants in the sixteenth century, which provokes Anderson to remark that this is 'a caution one might have thought all the more difficult to ignore a century later' (2004: 10). For Anderson, then, Nora's unwillingness to confront more troublesome and provocative aspects of French national history renders his project an anodyne and saccharine enterprise, merely 'the erudition of patriotic appeasement', and makes it 'one of the most patently ideological programmes in postwar historiography' (2004: 10).

A final omission from Nora's *Lieux de mémoire*, which has been remarked by Tony Judt, returns us to the opening of this section. It is clear that the experience and memory of war in the twentieth century has played a crucial role in France's fractured heritage. As Rousso elaborated, the memory of Vichy was cast into oblivion in 1945, forming a key site of national forgetting, and re-emerged only in the 1970s. The First World War also left deep scars in the French collective memory. Although not as morally troubling as the Second World War, the First World War nonetheless left five million men in France killed or wounded, hundreds of thousands of war widows and their children, and a shattered and devastated landscape in the north of the country, which, as Judt has pointed out, has only recently become the site of 'more confident commemoration' (1998: 57). More recently, France's 'dirty wars' in Indochina and Algeria carried mixed and ambivalent messages and memories. At a personal level, Nora's silence regarding war seems particularly curious. In addition to his youthful protests against the Algerian war, noted above, Nora has explicitly cited his childhood experiences as a Jew in wartime France as a powerful formative influence:

> When I was not yet ten years old, the war started, with the stunning spectacle of national collapse and the humiliation of foreign occupation. And since I was Jewish, I experienced exclusion, pursuit, the discovery of solidarities as unforeseen as the betrayals, and refuge with the Maquis in the Vercors. It was an adventure inscribed in the flesh of memory, sufficient to make you different from all other French children of your age.
>
> (Nora 2001: vii)

In light of the embeddedness of Nora's project in the crises of national identity surrounding Vichy, however, it is perhaps less surprising that, as Judt remarks, the memory of war 'deserves more attention than it receives in *Realms of Memory*' (1998: 57). In the next section, I aim precisely to pay close attention to the relation between war and collective memory. I seek to question, in particular, whether the nation represents the primary, or the most appropriate, vehicle for remembering or commemorating war. The section will begin by addressing Jay Winter's return to Halbwachs' emphasis on smaller memory communities, in his study of First World War memorialization. I will then focus on James Young's work on Holocaust memorials, which takes national remembering as its main focus, before questioning whether, in the current era of globalization, the notion of 'globalized' memory registers a new form of collective memory which is deserving of further scholarly attention, or whether it represents an expansion of the memory community beyond what can be considered as either practical or viable.

WAR AND COLLECTIVE MEMORY

Although the recent interest in collective memory can be traced to many sources, Jay Winter has justifiably noted the decisive contribution of war to the scholarship and debates in this area. Not only has the twentieth century been punctuated by warfare, Winter notes, but technological changes have ensured that war 'has moved out of the battlefield and into every corner of civilian life' (2006: 6). Witnesses of war, those who have experienced its effects at close range, whether as soldier or civilian, have contributed their memories to the historical record. Their stories have helped to shape how war is collectively remembered. In addition, the remembrance of the war dead can be regarded as an important impetus to the study of collective memory. Public commemorations and memorials to the dead are often caught between the state and other groups. Although the state tends towards narratives of valorization and sacrifice, celebrating moments of glory and heroism, individual or smaller group remembrances frequently emphasize lamentation or grief for those whose lives have been lost.

Winter's work explicitly contests Nora's emphasis on the nation as the primary vehicle for collective remembering. In *Sites of Memory, Sites of Mourning* (1995), Winter is critical of Nora's exclusive focus on 'Frenchness' and seeks to broaden his own study of 'sites of memory' to a more 'international' and 'comparative' emphasis (1995: 10). What Winter finds, through a comparison of the First World War memorials of three major combatant countries, Britain, France, and Germany, is a common vocabulary of loss, in which images and symbols were retrieved from the past in order to help people mourn. Winter accordingly departs from Nora's national framework in locating across all of these countries a 'common history of mourning' (1995: 10, 227). In *Remembering War* (2006), Winter's focus shifts to Halbwachs' work, and he is concerned to elucidate a history of collective remembering that is organized around the activities of smaller social groups. In the context of the First World War, Winter argues for the importance of shifting the scale of vision from grandiose national monuments to the more mundane and particular war memorials that commemorate the local dead in villages and towns. This change in focus brings to our attention that sites of memory are 'created not just by nations but primarily by small groups of men and women who do the work of remembrance' (2006: 136). Although, in line with Halbwachs, Winter's narrowing of vision brings to light the transience of collective memory, so that small groups dissolve when people 'lose interest, or time, or ... when they move away, or die' (2006: 4), it also emphasizes the agency and activism involved in memory work, which is initiated by a defined group of people in a specific place and for a particular reason. Winter's focus on the local war memorial also highlights a mode of commemoration that extends across western Europe, so that he again emphasizes, contrary to Nora, a transnational model of remembrance.

Winter's critique of Nora represents an important reminder that tropes of memory can cross not only national boundaries, but also the divide between victor and defeated. It is worth noting, however, that Winter's move away from the national framework is primarily connected to the remembrance of the First World War. The Second World War was less amenable to such approaches. Susan Suleiman has noted that every country involved in the later war 'has its own crises of memory not necessarily applicable to others' (2006: 3). As Martin Evans and Ken Lunn have argued, these national divisions of memory were brought into sharp focus by the international fiftieth-anniversary commemorations of the Second World War, which began in September 1989 and ended in August 1995 with the anniversary of the Victory over Japan Day. Each combatant nation staged commemorations of national significance: the British focused on the D-Day Landings, the Russians on Stalingrad, the Germans on the bombing of Dresden, and the Polish on the Warsaw Uprising. As the commemorative cycle progressed, however, it was marked by mounting acrimony. This tension was particularly apparent with the anniversary of the bombing of Hiroshima. Evans and Lunn outline the controversies surrounding this commemoration as follows:

> Calls from within Japan, demanding that the Allies should apologize, led to fury amongst Far East veterans in America, Britain and several other former dominions. For many of the latter, the atomic bomb was justified because it shortened the war and thus saved lives. And anyway, they went on, does not undue focus on Hiroshima risk forgetting the terrible atrocities carried out by Japanese militarism [the 'comfort women' of Korea and other conquered countries, the victims of the Burma railway, and the Nanking Massacre of December 1937] ? … Surely the Japanese government should be willing to acknowledge these aspects of war as well.
>
> (Evans and Lunn 1997: xv–xvi)

In addition to revealing confusion as to the intended purpose of remembering, whether it was to be celebratory or reflective, international or narrowly patriotic, these contestations demonstrated that even in the context of a single theatre of war, the Pacific conflict, memory of the event would be heavily dependent not only on victory or defeat, but also on whether the rememberer was American, British, Australian or Japanese: the tensions, in other words, merely underlined the significance of national perspective.

The Holocaust has become a particular focus of Second World War memorialization, to the extent that it has almost become a metonym for the conflict itself. As James Young has persuasively demonstrated, however, memories of the Holocaust are sharply divided along national lines. Noting that museums and memorials dedicated to the Holocaust 'remember events according to the hue of national ideals', Young resists the idea of a single, unitary memory of the Holocaust, asserting instead its plurality and multiplicity: 'the Shoah varies from land to land, political regime to political regime' (1993: viii). As Young goes on to demonstrate, German memorials recall the Jews by their absence and German victims by their political resistance; Polish memorials commemorate the whole of Polish destruction through the figure of the murdered Jews; Israel remembers the birth of the state through its martyrs and heroes; and American Holocaust memory is shaped by the distinctly American ideals of liberty, pluralism, and immigration. Young's work clearly owes much to Nora, yet he significantly also contests Nora's emphasis on national reconciliation. He points out that, once created, memorials 'take on lives of their own' and become invested with meanings that are 'stubbornly resistant to the state's original intentions' (1993: 3). Although Young emphasizes the importance of the nation in collective memorialization of the Holocaust, he is thus also mindful of the many layers and dimensions of national memory, so that he seeks 'to preserve the complex texture of memory – its many inconsistencies, faces, and shapes – that sustains the difficulty of memory work, not its easy resolution' (1993: xi).

More recently, as many critics have noted, the memory of the Holocaust has been transformed into a cipher for other collective traumas. The Holocaust has thus become a powerful lens through which we look at other instances of oppression and genocide. The emergence of the Holocaust as a template for collective suffering has led critics Daniel Levy and Natan Sznaider to consider whether we can justifiably speak of the Holocaust as constituting a new, global, cosmopolitan form of memory. The central question which underlies their work is whether, in the age of globalization, a new form of memory emerges which transcends national or ethnic boundaries and reflects a broader shared consciousness. Levy and Sznaider argue that the transformation in the significance of the Holocaust, so that it took on the role of a moral touchstone, took place in the 1990s against the historical backdrop of the Balkan crisis and unsuccessful demands for NATO intervention in Bosnia. The release of Steven Spielberg's *Schindler's List* in 1993 contributed to the universalization of the Holocaust by framing it as a moral story of good against evil. The film's clearly designated roles of good and evil resonated with emerging views of preventing genocide in the Balkans, and this connection was further reinforced at the inauguration of the United States Holocaust Memorial Museum, when the Holocaust survivor Elie Wiesel turned to President Clinton and called for military intervention in Bosnia. For Levy and Sznaider, then, the foundation for 'cosmopolitan' memories is provided by the emergence of international humanitarian organizations, such as NATO, and the concomitant diminution of national decision-making processes. These developments, they argue, entail that '[s]tate authority is being newly determined' and that '[n]ew transnational solidarities have the potential to emerge' (2002: 100). Their argument undoubtedly captures an important shift in the figuration of the Holocaust, so that it has now come to stand as a universal trope of traumatic history. I would nevertheless respond with a degree of caution to the concept of a 'global' Holocaust memory. Geoffrey Hartman has rightly observed that the multiple fracturing of the memory of the Holocaust in different countries has 'politically and culturally enabling aspects' and acts as 'a potential antidote to the freezing of memory into one traumatic image' (1993: 15). There is, then, much to be said for keeping the memory of the Holocaust local and site-specific, for it helps, as Hartman goes on to note, to 'make the Final Solution palpable' (1993: 16). I would also be wary of the inherent bias towards the First World, and specifically Europe, which underlies the prevalence of the Holocaust as trope. The 'globalization' of the Holocaust as a universal cipher of suffering is thus attended by the risk, as Margalit has pointed out, that 'the atrocities of Europe will come to be perceived as morally more significant than atrocities elsewhere', so that they come to claim 'false moral superiority' (2002: 80).

In this chapter, I have registered the fluctuating boundaries of the 'collective' across the key thinkers of the concept of collective memory. I have explored Halbwachs' emphasis on local and intimate memory communities, and discussed Winter's 'return' to Halbwachs in the context of First World War commemoration.

Nora's emphasis on the nation was subsequently developed and extended in Young's examination of the fracturing of Holocaust memory according to national myths and tropes. I ended by questioning whether it was possible to consider collective memory in an international context, focusing on Levy and Sznaider's concept of global or 'cosmopolitan' memory. I would like to conclude by briefly considering whether there is a 'natural' size for memory communities to function. In so doing, I propose to turn to Avishai Margalit's useful distinction between 'thick' and 'thin' relations. For him, 'thick relations' connect those with a shared past, and 'thin relations' connect those who are strangers or remote to each other. Margalit argues that the thick relations of family, ethnic, and religious groupings form the most natural communities of memory, for they are embedded in common experiences and events. Notably, although Margalit includes the nation within this category, Jay Winter contests his view, arguing that the maximum size at which a memory group can be effective 'falls well short of the nation' (2006: 137). Margalit addresses the notion of global memory by questioning whether there are certain shared memories that should be held in mind by humanity as a moral community. Although such a 'thin' notion of memory seems desirable to him, he points out that a single event does not have the same meaning for different communities, while there will also be an inevitable bias, in deciding which events to remember, towards the First World. Thus, although the conception of humanity as a global memory community remains an important aspiration, there are significant problems in constructing a shared moral memory for mankind. Margalit's concept of 'thick relations' returns us to Halbwachs' insight that collective remembering is not only, or even primarily, concerned with preserving the past but rather with maintaining social cohesion and identity. For this reason, although there are associated hazards of nostalgia, sacralization, and parochialism, the most promising work on collective memory seems to be that which is concerned with more intimate, 'thick' relations, and smaller, more intimately connected groups appear to constitute more 'natural' communities for collective remembering.

CONCLUSION
The art of forgetting?

Since the Second World War, there has been a proliferation of memory work. This trend has noticeably intensified since the 1980s, and the last decade or so has witnessed the inauguration of an ever increasing number of museums and memorials to human suffering. In line with Nora, it is possible to question whether this 'memory work' itself constitutes a form of forgetting, so that we delegate the responsibility for remembering to the memorials and museums that we are so keen to erect. It has also been notable, however, that the last few years have witnessed an accelerated fashion for scenes of public repentance, forgiveness, apology, or confession. This has been manifested through a series of gestures by heads of state. We have thus seen British Prime Minister Tony Blair apologize for his country's role in the Irish potato famine from 1845 to 1851; the Australian institution of an annual Sorry Day to commemorate the government's stealing of some 100,000 Aboriginal children from their parents to be raised by white families; the Canadian government's apology to its native indigenous population for past actions suppressing their languages, cultures, and spiritual practices; and the Japanese Prime Minister's apology for suffering inflicted in the Second World War. These years have also seen the institution of a number of Truth Commissions, which have taken place in South Africa, Chile, Guatemala, and Argentina. These phenomena respond to a growing public interest in restorative justice and aim to promote healing and reconciliation in the aftermath of political violence. Taken together, however, they also suggest that a discursive shift is beginning to take place from memory to forgetting. They engage us with the question of when forgetting becomes salutary, even necessary, but they also give rise to related questions concerning the relation between forgetting and forgiving, and whether we can speak of a collective forgetting as well as a collective remembering. In conclusion to this volume, I would therefore like to address these issues by briefly discussing the important work on forgetting that has recently emerged; namely, Jacques Derrida's 'On Forgiveness' (2001b) and the last section of Paul Ricoeur's final work *Memory, History, Forgetting* (2004).

Derrida articulates a clear scepticism concerning the recent 'globalisation' of forgiveness, which combines a renewed discourse of human rights with 'a process of Christianisation' to produce 'an immense scene of confession' (2001b: 31). Although the language of apology adopted is that of the 'Abrahamic' (Jewish, Christian, Islamic) tradition, Derrida notes that, in the cases of Japan and Korea in particular, the gesture extends to cultures that are totally foreign to that religion (2001b: 28). Forgiveness, then, has become a universal idiom of politics, law, and diplomacy, and in this context, it has become inextricable from strategic calculations and conditions, and is, Derrida argues, 'taken far too lightly' (2001b: 41). In opposition to this dilution and diminution of the concept of forgiveness, Derrida proposes a 'mad' or 'impossible' version of forgiveness that forgives only the unforgivable. He confronts us with an aporia, forgiveness without condition, which aims to resituate forgiveness outside of the political and juridical process and in relation to the 'unconditional purity' of the divine (2001b: 39, 44). However, Derrida also crucially argues that such an excessive notion of pure forgiveness is, at the same time, inseparable from the political order; if forgiveness is to become effective, to have concrete historical results, its purity must engage itself in a series of conditions (political, juridical, social). For Derrida, then, forgiveness is suspended between two irreconcilable but indissociable poles, '*the unconditional and the conditional*', which represent, respectively, the impossible but necessary aspiration towards pure forgiveness and the reality of human society (2001b: 44, original emphasis).

Paul Ricoeur engages closely with Derrida's two modes of forgiveness and relates them, in turn, to the question of forgetting. For Ricoeur, Derrida's pure forgiveness corresponds to a definitive forgetting, which he terms a 'forgetting through the erasing of traces'; forgiveness in its unattainable, ideal (divine) sense thus overcomes all traces of the act to be forgiven. The more human, conditional form of forgiveness is equated by Ricoeur with what he terms 'a forgetting in reserve'; this is a forgiveness which disregards the original act rather than erasing it entirely (2004: 414). Ricoeur initially concurs with Derrida that forgiveness should be directed towards the unconditional, forgetting through the erasing of traces, even if this is impossible. However, he also crucially goes on to point out that this category of forgiveness is more troubling if it is considered on the collective rather than on the individual level. Ricoeur thus translates the terms of individual experience, 'forgiving' and 'forgetting', into the more juridical or collective pairing of 'amnesty' and 'amnesia'. The substitution of 'amnesia' for 'forgetting' troubles Ricoeur, because it introduces into his discussion, as Susan Suleiman has noted, 'an illness – or worse still, an alibi' (2006: 217). Although the stated intention of amnesty is reconciliation or civil peace, Ricoeur notes that its linguistic proximity to amnesia acts as a salutary reminder of its potential hazards: '[t]he proximity, which is more than phonetic … signals the existence of a secret pact with the denial of memory, which … distances [amnesty] from forgiving' (2004: 453). As Ricoeur goes on to note, in an observation which is particularly relevant to Rousso's elaboration of the 'forgetting' of Vichy in France following the legal amnesties of wartime collaborators in the 1950s, this aspect of amnesty is especially pronounced under French law, which makes it a crime to allude to someone's past if those activities fall under a law of amnesty, and shuts down

archives that contain traces of those activities. Ricoeur unequivocally notes that this 'amounts to extinguishing memory ... and
to saying that nothing has occurred' (2004: 455). In the realm of
collective forgetting, then, unconditional forgiveness, forgetting
through the erasing of traces, assumes a noticeably more troubling
aspect than when it is conceived on the individual level.

Although Ricoeur and Derrida thus differ in perspective with
regard to certain issues, both thinkers struggle with the uncomfortable but necessary distinctions between forgetting without
amnesia, and forgiving without erasing memory. Ricoeur concludes his volume by bringing us back full circle to the 'art of
memory' elaborated by Frances Yates. He questions whether it
would be possible to develop an 'art of forgetting', which would
work in strict symmetry with the 'art of memory', so that it
formed a technique not of memorization but of extinction (2004:
504). Ricoeur's question has been answered, in part, by Harald
Weinrich, who considers whether such a 'lethotechnics' would
indeed be desirable (2004: 12). In so doing, he tells an alternative
narrative of Simonides to the story which I cited in Chapter 1.
According to Cicero, Simonides approached the politician and
military leader Themistocles and offered to teach him the art of
memory, so that he might be able to remember everything. In
response, Themistocles replied that he had no need of an art of
memory and would prefer to learn how to forget everything that
he wanted to forget. Cicero informs us that Themistocles pre-
ferred an 'art of forgetting' only because he already possessed an
excellent natural memory, which retained too much rather than
too little. In Cicero's anecdote, then, forgetting figures primarily
as a practical problem, concerned with erasing some of the traces
that have been inscribed onto the tablet of memory. For Weinrich,
however, contemporary forgetting represents more of an ethical or
moral problem. In the light of twentieth-century crimes against
humanity, he concludes that he cannot subscribe to the barbarous
dream of an 'art of forgetting': 'forgetting is no longer allowed'
(2004: 184). I would like to conclude, however, by suggesting
that we dwell a little longer with the possibility of forgetting. It
seems to me that forgetting, *considered in all of its complexity*, deserves
to be taken seriously, both because it is an inseparable and not

always sufficiently recognized aspect of memory itself, and because some measure of forgetting is a necessary requirement for personal and civic health. Although I would like to register the importance of the cultural specificity of Weinrich's position as a German post-Holocaust philosopher, I therefore propose to close by countering him, and by arguing that a mode of forgetting *which holds the past in reserve* is not only possible ('allowed') but also to some extent desirable; that forgetting, paradoxical as it may seem, constitutes a crucial if not essential element in the future trajectory and direction of 'memory' studies.

GLOSSARY

Abreaction In psychoanalysis, the release and discharge of emotional tension which has become **overcathected** or built up around a traumatic event. The abreaction of the affect means that it is not able to become (or to remain) pathogenic. Abreaction can either be provoked in the course of psychoanalysis or come about spontaneously, either a short time or a long time after the original traumatic event.

Anamnesis The recollection of things past. For Plato, the doctrine according to which the soul has pre-existed in a purer state and there gained its Ideas.

Art of memory After the Latin *ars memoriae* and commonly used in the titles of works on **mnemonics** in the late fifteenth and early sixteenth centuries. The phrase refers to a system of **mnemonic** devices.

Cabalism The term derives from an ancient Jewish mystical tradition, but it refers by extension to any secret or occult doctrine.

Collective memory Most commonly associated with Maurice Halbwachs; collective memory refers to a memory or set of memories that are shared, passed on, and constructed by the group, as opposed to an individual subject. More recent scholars have built on the work of Halbwachs. Paul Connerton has explored the human body as a site for collective memory processes, while James E. Young has proposed that we refer to 'collected memory' rather than 'collective memory' because groups and societies can remember only through their constituents' memories.

Condensation In psychoanalysis, this describes one of the central modes of functioning of the unconscious processes. A single idea represents or 'condenses' several chains of association, at whose point of intersection it is located. Condensation can be seen at work in the symptom and in dreams, and it accounts for the exceptional intensity of certain images and ideas.

Dialectic In philosophy, the art of reasoning or disputation by question and answer, associated particularly with Plato.

Dissociation In psychiatry, this refers to the separation of a group of mental processes or ideas from the rest of the personality, so that they lead an independent existence, and the disintegration of consciousness that results.

Empiricism The philosophical doctrine that all knowledge derives from experience and observation rather than from theory or speculation.

Habit memory For Henri Bergson, the obtaining of certain forms of automatic behaviour by means of repetition. Habit memory is aligned for Bergson with bodily perception and coincides with the acquisition of sensorimotor mechanisms. For this reason, it contrasts unfavourably for Bergson with **pure memory**.

Hermeticism A body of knowledge relating to Hermes Trismegistus and, by extension, to alchemy and other forms of ancient science. Hermes Trismegistus (Hermes thrice-greatest) was the name given by the **Neoplatonists** and the devotees of mysticism and alchemy to the Egyptian god Thoth, who was in turn closely associated with the Grecian Hermes, regarded as the author of all mysterious doctrines and especially the secrets of alchemy.

Hippocampus A brain structure which lies under the medial temporal lobe. It plays an important part in long-term memory and spatial navigation. In Alzheimer's disease, the hippocampus is one of the first regions of the brain to show damage; memory problems and dislocation appear among the first symptoms. Damage to the hippocampus can also result in the loss of ability to form new memories, although older memories may be unaffected.

Involuntary memory In Marcel Proust's *A la recherche du temps perdu* [In Search of Lost Time], this refers to a conception of human memory in which external cues evoke recollections of the past, and which is thereby highly sensory and physical. The most famous instance of involuntary memory is the episode of the madeleine, although there are a number of other sequences of involuntary memory in Proust's novel. Involuntary memory is distinguished by Proust from **voluntary memory**.

Memory place Deriving from the Latin *loci memoriae*, the memory place refers to an internalized place, which could be either remembered or imagined. It most commonly comprised a building divided into various rooms and areas, each containing mnemonic objects and features that symbolized particular ideas and were visualized mentally as a way of remembering those ideas. This form of mnemonic device was commonly recommended in ancient, medieval, and early-modern memory treatises and handbooks.

Memory theatre A portable wooden theatre into which about two people could enter at any one time. The most famous example was made by Giulio Camillo (1480–1544). Drawing on the tradition of the **memory place**, the memory theatre integrated architecture and imagery to reflect the emerging **Hermetic** philosophy of the Renaissance. The theatre acted as a mnemonic aid or device for recollecting the divine order.

Mnemonics The study and development of systems for assisting and improving the memory. These systems may employ various techniques or aids, such as visualization or the use of rhythm and rhyme.

Mnemosyne In ancient Greek myth, the goddess of memory and the mother by Zeus of the nine Muses, including Clio, the goddess of History.

Neoplatonism A philosophical system that developed in the third century AD as a synthesis of Platonic, Pythagorean, and Aristotelian elements with oriental mysticism. It emphasized the distinction between an eternal world accessible to thought and the changing physical world accessible to the senses, and combined this with a mystical belief in the possibility of union with a supreme being from whom all reality was thought to derive. Neoplatonism was an important influence on early Christian writers and on later medieval and Renaissance thought.

Overcathected In psychoanalysis, cathexis refers to the economic concept that a certain amount of psychical energy is attached to an idea or a group of ideas, to a part of the body or to an object. The subject thus draws on a specific quantity of energy which she distributes in varying proportions in her relationships with objects and with herself. Overcathexis arises when an object, idea, or body part is invested with an excess of psychical energy, for example in mourning when there is an over-attachment of energies in relation to the lost object.

Pure memory For Henri Bergson, the survival of personal memories in the unconscious. Pure memory is distinguished by Bergson from **habit memory**.

Rhetoric The body of rules to be observed by a speaker or orator in order that he may express himself with eloquence. In the classical period, rhetoric was considered an 'art' and was integral to the activity of speech-making. The five parts of rhetoric were: invention, disposition, style, memory, and delivery. In the medieval period, rhetoric was considered one of the seven 'liberal arts' and was included, along with grammar and logic, in the 'trivium'.

Scholasticism The system of philosophy, theology, and teaching that dominated Europe between AD 1000 and 1500. It was based on the authority of the Christian Fathers and on the writing of Aristotle and his commentators.

Screen memory A psychoanalytic concept first elaborated by Freud in 1899. A screen memory is a compromise between repressed elements and defences against them. Recollections of this kind are characterized both by their clarity and by the apparent insignificance of their content. Important facts are not retained; instead, their psychic significance is displaced onto closely associated but less important details.

Sites of memory Coined by Pierre Nora, sites of memory *lieux de mémoire* is a translation into French of **memory places** (*loci memoriae*). For Nora, a site of memory is any significant entity, material or immaterial, which has become a symbolic element of the memorial heritage of a community. Sites of memory are where culture crystallizes itself, and can include places such as archives, museums, or memorials; concepts or practices such as commemorative rituals; objects such as emblems or manuals; and symbols. In his seven-volume study of sites of memory *Les Lieux de mémoire* (1984–92) Nora identified and analysed the key sites of memory of the French nation.

Voluntary memory In Proust, this refers to memories that are retrieved when we put a conscious effort into recollecting events, people, and places. For Proust, voluntary memories contrast unfavourably with **involuntary memories** which capture the 'essence' of the past.

BIBLIOGRAPHY

Anderson, Perry (2004) 'Union Sucrée', *London Review of Books*, 23 September, pp. 10–16.

Aristotle (1972) 'De Memoria et Reminiscentia', in Richard Sorabji (trans. and ed.), *Aristotle on Memory*, London: Duckworth, pp. 47–60.

Assmann, Jan (1995) 'Collective Memory and Cultural Identity', trans. John Czaplicka, *New German Critique* 65: 125–33.

Augé, Marc (2004) *Oblivion*, trans. Marjolijn de Jager, foreword by James E.Young, Minneapolis and London: University of Minnesota Press.

Augustine, St (1961) *Confessions*, trans. R. S. Pine-Coffin, Harmondsworth: Penguin.

Bal, Mieke (2002) *Travelling Concepts in the Humanities: A Rough Guide*, Toronto, Buffalo, and London: University of Toronto Press.

Beckett, Samuel (1931) *Proust*, New York and London: Grove Press.

Benjamin, Walter (1970) *Illuminations*, ed. and intro. by Hannah Arendt, trans. Harry Zohn, London: Jonathan Cape.

Bergson, Henri (1991) *Matter and Memory*, trans. N. M. Paul and W. S. Palmer, New York: Zone Books.

Bromwich, David (1998) *Disowned by Memory: Wordsworth's Poetry of the 1790s*, Chicago and London: University of Chicago Press.

Carruthers, Mary (1990) *The Book of Memory: A Study of Memory in Medieval Culture*, Cambridge and New York: Cambridge University Press.

Caruth, Cathy (1995a) 'Trauma and Experience: Introduction', in Cathy Caruth (ed.), *Trauma: Explorations in Memory*, Baltimore and London: Johns Hopkins University Press, pp. 3–12.

——(1995b) 'Recapturing the Past: Introduction', in Cathy Caruth (ed.), *Trauma: Explorations in Memory*, Baltimore and London: Johns Hopkins University Press, pp. 151–7.

Casey, Edward S. (1987) *Remembering: A Phenomenological Study*, second edn, Bloomington, IL and Indianapolis: Indiana University Press.

Chedgzoy, Kate (2007) *Women's Writing in the British Atlantic World: Memory, Place and History, 1550–1700*, Cambridge and New York: Cambridge University Press.

[Cicero, Marcus Tullius] (1954) *Ad Herennium*, trans. Harry Caplan, Loeb Classical Library, Cambridge, MA and London: Harvard University Press.

——(2001) *On the Ideal Orator*, trans. with introduction, notes, appendixes, glossary, and indexes by James M. May and Jakob Wisse, New York and Oxford: Oxford University Press.

Coleman, Janet (1992) *Ancient and Medieval Memories*, Cambridge and New York: Cambridge University Press.

Connerton, Paul (1989) *How Societies Remember*, Cambridge and New York: Cambridge University Press.

Coser, Lewis A. (1992) 'Introduction: Maurice Halbwachs 1877–1945', in Maurice Halbwachs, *On Collective Memory*, ed., trans., and intro. Lewis A. Coser, Chicago and London: University of Chicago Press.

Craig, Edward (1998) 'Memory', in Edward Craig (ed.), *Routledge Encyclopedia of Philosophy*, London: Routledge, vol. 6, pp. 296–300.

Dante (1970) *The Divine Comedy: Inferno 1: Italian Text and Translation*, trans. with a commentary by Charles S. Singleton, Bollingen Series LXXX, Princeton, NJ: Princeton University Press.

——(1975) *The Divine Comedy: Paradiso 1: Italian Text and Translation*, trans. with a commentary by Charles S. Singleton, Bollingen Series LXXX, Princeton, NJ: Princeton University Press.

de Man, Paul (1979) 'Excuses (Confessions)', in *Allegories of Reading: Figural Language in Rousseau, Nietzsche, Rilke, and Proust*, New Haven, CT and London: Yale University Press, pp. 278–302.

Delbo, Charlotte (1990) *Days and Memory*, trans. Rosette Lamont, Marlboro, VT: The Marlboro Press.

Derrida, Jacques (1981) 'Plato's Pharmacy', in *Dissemination*, trans. Barbara Johnson, Chicago: University of Chicago Press, pp. 61–172.

——(1989) *Memoires for Paul de Man*, rev. edn., trans. Cecile Lindsay, Jonathan Culler, Eduardo Cadava, and Peggy Kamuf, ed. Avital Ronell and Eduardo Cadava, New York: Columbia University Press.

——(2001a) 'Freud and the Scene of Writing', in *Writing and Difference*, trans. Alan Bass, London and New York: Routledge, pp. 246–91.

——(2001b) 'On Forgiveness', in *Cosmopolitanism and Forgiveness*, trans. Mark Dooley and Michael Hughes, pref. by Simon Critchley and Richard Kearnley, London and New York: Routledge.

Dienstag, Joshua Foa (1997) *Dancing in Chains: Narrative and Memory in Political Theory*, Stanford: Stanford University Press.

Douglas, Mary (1980) 'Introduction: Maurice Halbwachs (1877–1945)', in Maurice Halbwachs, *The Collective Memory*, trans. Francis J. Ditter and Vida Yazdi Ditter, New York and London: Harper and Row, pp. 1–21.

Draaisma, Douwe (2000) *Metaphors of Memory: A History of Ideas about the Mind*, trans. Paul Vincent, Cambridge and New York: Cambridge University Press.

Durkheim, Emile (2001) *The Elementary Forms of Religious Life*, trans. Carol Closman, abridged with an intro. and notes by Mark S. Cladis, Oxford and New York: Oxford University Press.

Evans, Martin and Ken Lunn (1997), 'Preface', in Martin Evans and Ken Lunn (eds), *War and Memory in the Twentieth Century*, Oxford and New York: Berg.

Ferguson, Frances (1996) 'Romantic Memory', *Studies in Romanticism* 35: 509–33.

Freud, Sigmund (2001) *The Standard Edition of the Complete Psychological Works of Sigmund Freud* (24 vols), trans. and ed. James Strachey in collaboration with Anna Freud, assisted by Alix Strachey and Alan Tyson, London: Vintage.

Fritzsche, Peter (2004) *Stranded in the Present: Modern Time and the Melancholy of History*, Cambridge, MA and London: Harvard University Press.

Frow, John (1997) *Time and Commodity Culture: Essays in Cultural Theory and Postmodernity*, Oxford: Clarendon Press.

Gedi, Noa and Yigal Elam (1996) 'Collective Memory – What Is It?', *History and Memory* 8.1: 30–50.

Goody, Jack and Ian Watt (1968) 'The Consequences of Literacy', in J. R. Goody (ed.), *Literacy in Traditional Societies*, Cambridge and New York: Cambridge University Press, pp. 27–68.

Grant, Linda (1998) *Remind Me Who I Am, Again*, London: Granta.

Haaken, Janice (1998) *Pillar of Salt: Gender, Memory and the Perils of Looking Back*, New Brunswick, NJ and London: Rutgers University Press.

Halbwachs, Maurice (1980) *The Collective Memory*, trans. Francis J. Ditter and Vida Yazdi Ditter, intro. Mary Douglas, New York: Harper and Row.

——(1992) *On Collective Memory*, ed., trans., and intro. Lewis A. Coser, Chicago and London: University of Chicago Press.

Hartle, Ann (1983) *The Modern Self in Rousseau's Confessions: A Reply to St. Augustine*, Notre Dame, IN: University of Notre Dame Press.

Hartman, Geoffrey H. (1993) 'Introduction: Darkness Visible', in Geoffrey H. Hartman (ed.), *Holocaust Remembrance: The Shapes of Memory*, Oxford and Cambridge, MA: Blackwell, pp. 1–22.

Havelock, Eric A. (1963) *Preface to Plato*, Cambridge, MA and London: Harvard University Press.

Hirsch, Marianne and Valerie Smith (2002) 'Feminism and Cultural Memory: An Introduction', *Signs: Journal of Women in Culture and Society* 28.1: 3–12.

Hume, David (2000) *A Treatise of Human Nature*, ed. David Fate Norton and Mary J. Norton, Oxford: Oxford University Press.

Huyssen, Andreas (1995) *Twilight Memories: Marking Time in a Culture of Amnesia*, New York and London: Routledge.

Johnson, Christopher (1993) *System and Writing in the Philosophy of Jacques Derrida*, Cambridge and New York: Cambridge University Press.

Jordan, Jack (2001) 'The Unconscious', in Richard Bales (ed.), *The Cambridge Companion to Proust*, Cambridge: Cambridge University Press, pp. 100–16.

Judt, Tony (1998) 'A La Recherche du Temps Perdu', *New York Review of Books*, 3 December, pp. 51–8.

Kansteiner, Wulf (2002) 'Finding Meaning in Memory: A Methodological Critique of Memory Studies', *History and Theory* 41: 179–97.

Kaplan, Brett Ashley (2001) 'Pleasure, Memory, and Time Suspension in Holocaust Literature: Celan and Delbo', *Comparative Literature Studies* 38.4: 310–29.

Klein, Kerwin Lee (2000) 'On the Emergence of *Memory* in Historical Discourse', *Representations* 69: 127–50.

Krell, David Farrell (1990) *Of Memory, Reminiscence and Writing: On the Verge*, Bloomington, IN: Indiana University Press.

Kristeva, Julia (1993) *Proust and the Sense of Time*, trans. Stephen Bann, New York: Columbia University Press.

Kritzman, Lawrence D. (1996) 'Foreword', in Pierre Nora, *Realms of Memory: Rethinking the French Past*, English language edn, ed. Lawrence D.

Kritzman, trans. Arthur Goldhammer, New York: Columbia University Press, vol. I, pp. ix–xiv.

Kuhn, Annette (2002) *Family Secrets: Acts of Memory and Imagination*, London: Verso.

Kundera, Milan (1984) *The Unbearable Lightness of Being*, trans. Michael Henry Heim, London: Faber.

LaCapra, Dominick (2001) *Writing History, Writing Trauma*, Baltimore and London: Johns Hopkins University Press.

Laplanche, Jean and J.-B. Pontalis (1988) *The Language of Psycho-Analysis*, trans. Donald Nicholson-Smith, intro. Daniel Lagache, London: Karnac and the Institute of Psychoanalysis.

Le Goff, Jacques (1992) *History and Memory*, trans. Steven Rendall and Elizabeth Claman, New York: Columbia University Press.

Levy, Daniel and Natan Sznaider (2002) 'Memory Unbound: The Holocaust and the Formation of Cosmopolitan Memory', *European Journal of Social Theory* 5.1: 87–106.

Leydersdorff, Selma, Luisa Passerini, and Paul Thompson (2005) *Gender and Memory*, New Brunswick, NJ and London: Transaction Publishers.

Leys, Ruth (2000) *Trauma: A Genealogy*, Chicago and London: Chicago University Press.

Locke, John (1996) *Some Thoughts Concerning Education and Of the Conduct of the Understanding*, ed. Ruth W. Grant and Nathan Tarcov, Indianapolis, IN and Cambridge, MA: Hackett Publishing.

——(1997) *An Essay Concerning Human Understanding*, ed. Roger Woolhouse, London and New York: Penguin.

Lowenthal, David (1996) *Possessed by the Past: The Heritage Crusade and the Spoils of History*, New York: Free Press.

Luria, A. R. (1987) *The Mind of a Mnemonist: A Little Book about a Vast Memory*, trans. Lynn Solotaroff, Cambridge, MA and London: Harvard University Press. First published in 1968.

Maier, Charles (1993) 'A Surfeit of Memory: Reflections on History, Melancholy and Denial', *History and Memory* 5.2: 136–52.

Marcus, Laura (1994) *Auto/biographical Discourses: Theory, Criticism, Practice*, Manchester and New York: Manchester University Press.

Margalit, Avishai (2002) *The Ethics of Memory*, Cambridge, MA and London: Harvard University Press.

May, James M. and Jakob Wisse (2001) 'Introduction', in James M. May and Jakob Wisse, *Cicero: On the Ideal Orator*, New York and Oxford: Oxford University Press, pp. 3–48.

Nietzsche, Friedrich Wilhelm (1997) 'On the Uses and Disadvantages of History for Life', in Daniel Breazale (ed.), *Untimely Meditations*, trans. R. J. Hollingdale, Cambridge: Cambridge University Press.

Nora, Pierre (ed.) (1996–98) *Realms of Memory: Rethinking the French Past*, English language edn, ed. and foreword Lawrence D. Kritzman, trans. Arthur Goldhammer, 3 vols, New York: Columbia University Press.

———(2001) 'General Introduction', trans. Richard C. Holbrook, in *Rethinking France: Les Lieux de Mémoire*, vol. 1: *The State*, trans. Mary Trouille, Chicago and London: University of Chicago Press, pp. vii–xii.

Nussbaum, Felicity (1989) *The Autobiographical Subject: Gender and Ideology in Eighteenth-Century England*, Baltimore and London: Johns Hopkins University Press.

Pfau, Thomas (2005) *Romantic Moods: Paranoia, Trauma, and Melancholy, 1790-1840*, Baltimore and London: Johns Hopkins University Press.

Plato (1956) *Protagoras and Meno*, trans. W. K. C. Guthrie, Harmondsworth: Penguin.

———(1987) *Theaetetus*, trans. Robin A. H. Waterfield, Harmondsworth: Penguin.

———(2005) *Phaedrus*, trans. Christopher Rowe, Harmondsworth: Penguin.

Proust, Marcel (2002) *In Search of Lost Time*, trans. C. K. Scott Moncrieff and Terence Kilmartin, rev. by D. J. Enright, 6 vols, London: Vintage.

Quintilian (1979), *Institutio Oratoria IV*, trans. H. E. Butler, Loeb Classical Library, Cambridge, MA and London: Harvard University Press and William Heinemann.

Radstone, Susannah (2000) 'Working with Memory: An Introduction', in *Memory and Methodology*, ed. Susannah Radstone, Oxford and New York: Berg, pp. 1–24.

Rajan, Tilottama (1980) *Dark Interpreter: The Discourse of Romanticism*, Ithaca, NY: Cornell University Press.

———(1990) *The Supplement of Reading: Figures of Understanding in Romantic Theory and Practice*, Ithaca, NY: Cornell University Press.

Reading, Anna (2002) *The Social Inheritance of the Holocaust: Gender, Culture and Memory*, Basingstoke and New York: Palgrave Macmillan.

Ricoeur, Paul (2004) *Memory, History, Forgetting*, trans. Kathleen Blamey and David Pellauer, Chicago and London: University of Chicago Press.

Rossington, Michael (2007a) 'Introduction: Enlightenment and Romantic Memory', in Michael Rossington and Anne Whitehead (eds), *Theories of Memory: A Reader*, Edinburgh: Edinburgh University Press, pp. 70–4.

———(2007b) 'Introduction: Collective Memory', in Michael Rossington and Anne Whitehead (eds), *Theories of Memory: A Reader*, Edinburgh: Edinburgh University Press, pp. 134–8.

Rousseau, Jean-Jacques (1953) *The Confessions*, trans. and introd. by J. M. Cohen, London and New York: Penguin.

Rousso, Henry (1991) *The Vichy Syndrome: History and Memory in France Since 1944*, trans. Arthur Goldhammer, Cambridge, MA and London: Harvard University Press.

Samuel, Raphael (1994) *Theatres of Memory*, vol. 1: *Past and Present in Contemporary Culture*, London and New York: Verso.

Santner, Eric L. (2006) *On Creaturely Life: Rilke, Benjamin, Sebald*, Chicago and London: University of Chicago Press.

Semprún, Jorge (1997) *Literature or Life*, trans. Linda Coverdale, Harmondsworth: Penguin.

Shattuck, Roger (2001) 'Lost and Found: The Structure of Proust's Novel', in Richard Bales (ed.), *The Cambridge Companion to Proust*, Cambridge: Cambridge University Press, pp. 74–84.

Sheringham, Michael (1993) *French Autobiography: Devices and Desires: Rousseau to Perec*, Oxford: Clarendon Press.

Sorabji, Richard (1972) *Aristotle on Memory*, London: Duckworth.

Starobinski, Jean (1988) *Jean-Jacques Rousseau: Transparency and Obstruction*, trans. Arthur Goldhammer, intro. Robert J. Morrissey, Chicago and London: University of Chicago Press.

Stewart, Victoria (2003) *Women's Autobiography: War and Trauma*, Basingstoke: Palgrave Macmillan.

Strickland, Geoffrey (1988) 'The Analysis of Memory', *The Cambridge Quarterly* 17.4: 386–97.

Sturken, Marita (1997) *Tangled Memories: The Vietnam War, the AIDS Epidemic and the Politics of Remembering*, Berkeley, CA: University of California Press.

Suleiman, Susan Rubin (2006) *Crises of Memory and the Second World War*, Cambridge, MA and London: Harvard University Press.

Terdiman, Richard (1993) *Present Past: Modernity and the Memory Crisis*, Ithaca, NY and London: Cornell University Press.

van der Kolk, Bessel and Onno van der Hart (1995) 'The Intrusive Past: The Flexibility of Memory and the Engraving of Trauma', in Cathy Caruth (ed.), *Trauma: Explorations in Memory*, Baltimore and London: Johns Hopkins University Press, pp. 158–82.

Warnock, Mary (1987) *Memory*, London: Faber.

Weinrich, Harald (2004) *Lethe: The Art and Critique of Forgetting*, trans. Steven Rendall, Ithaca, NY and London: Cornell University Press.

Williams, Huntington (1983) *Rousseau and Romantic Autobiography*, Oxford and New York: Oxford University Press.

Winter, Jay (1995) *Sites of Memory, Sites of Mourning*, Cambridge: Cambridge University Press.

——(2006) *Remembering War: The Great War Between History and Memory in the Twentieth Century*, New Haven, CT, and London: Yale University Press.

Wood, Nancy (1999) *Vectors of Memory: Legacies of Trauma in Postwar Europe*, Oxford and New York: Berg.

Wordsworth, William (1991) 'Lines Written a Few Miles Above Tintern Abbey, On Revisiting the Banks of the Wye During a Tour, July 13, 1798', in R. L. Brett and R. Jones (eds), *Lyrical Ballads*, second edn, Oxford and New York: Routledge, pp. 113–18.

Yates, Frances A. (1966) *The Art of Memory*, London: Routledge and Kegan Paul.

Yerushalmi, Yosef Hayim (1996) *Zakhor: Jewish History and Jewish Memory*, Seattle and London: University of Washington Press. First published in 1982.

Yolton, John W. (1970) *Locke and the Compass of Human Understanding: A Selective Commentary on the Essay*, Cambridge: Cambridge University Press.

Young, Allan (1997) *The Harmony of Illusions: Inventing Post-Traumatic Stress Disorder*, Princeton, NJ: Princeton University Press.

Young, James E. (1993) *The Texture of Memory: Holocaust Memorials and Meaning*, New Haven, CT and London: Yale University Press.

INDEX

Related titles from Routledge

Critical Theory Today

Second Edition

Lois Tyson

This new edition of the classic guide offers a thorough and accessible
introduction to contemporary critical theory. It provides in-depth
coverage of the most common approaches to literary analysis today:
feminism, psychoanalysis, Marxism, reader-response theory, new
criticism, structuralism and semiotics, deconstruction, new historicism,
cultural criticism, lesbian/gay/queer theory, African-American
criticism, and postcolonial criticism. The chapters provide an
extended explanation of each theory, using examples from everyday life, popular culture, and literary texts; a list of specific questions critics who use that theory ask about literary texts; an
interpretation of F. Scott Fitzgerald's *The Great Gatsby* through the
lens of each theory; a list of questions for further practice to guide
readers in applying each theory to different literary works; and a
bibliography of primary and secondary works for further reading.
This book can be used as the only text in a course or as a precursor to
the study of primary theoretical works. It motivates readers by
showing them what critical theory can offer in terms of their practical
understanding of literary texts and in terms of their personal understanding of themselves and the world in which they live. Both
engaging and rigorous, it is a 'how-to' book for undergraduate and
graduate students new to critical theory and for college professors
who want to broaden their repertoire of critical approaches to literature.

ISBN 13: 978-0-415-97409-7 (hbk)
ISBN 13: 978-0-415-97410-3 (pbk)

The Routledge Critical and Cultural Theory Reader

Edited by Neil Badmington and Julia Thomas

Everything is open to question. Nothing is sacred.

Critical and cultural theory invites a rethinking of some of our most basic assumptions about who we are, how we behave, and how we interpret the world around us.

The Routledge Critical and Cultural Theory Reader brings together 29 key pieces from the last century and a half that have shaped the field. Topics include: subjectivity, language, gender, ethnicity, sexuality, the body, the human, class, culture, everyday life, literature, psychoanalysis, technology, power, and visuality. The choice of texts, together with the editors' introduction and glossary, will allow newcomers to begin from first principles, while the use of unabridged readings will also make the volume suitable for those undertaking more specialized work. Material is arranged chronologically, but the editors have suggested thematic pathways through the selections.

Contributors include key figures in critical theory and cultural studies:

Giorgio Agamben, Gloria Anzaldúa, Roland Barthes, Jean Baudrillard, Walter Benjamin, Lauren Berlant, Judith Butler, Michel de Certeau, Gilles Deleuze, Jacques Derrida, Frantz Fanon, Michel Foucault, Sigmund Freud, Marjorie Garber, Félix Guattari, Stuart Hall, Donna J Haraway, Julia Kristeva, Jacques Lacan, Henri Lefebvre, Jean-François Lyotard, Karl Marx, Chandra Talpade Mohanty, Laura Mulvey, Joan Riviere, Gayle Rubin, Edward Said, Ferdinand de Saussure, Michael Warner, Hayden White and Raymond Williams.

ISBN 13: 978-0-415-43308-2 (hbk)
ISBN 13: 978-0-415-43309-9 (pbk)

Available at all good bookshops
For ordering and further information please visit:
www.routledge.com

Culture and the Real
Theorizing Cultural Criticism

Catherine Belsey

New Accents

'Belsey is that rarest of birds, a tough-minded romantic, at once a close reader and a far-seeker. She has shown us all how it is possible to write with extraordinary methodological and theoretical sophistication, and at the same time to write clearly, gracefully, and simply. Belsey demonstrates by example that criticism can go about its academic business and still demand the critic to examine and take position on issues that affect our lives.'

Harry Berger, Professor of Literature and Art History,
University of California, Santa Cruz

What makes us the people we are? Culture evidently plays a part, but how large a part? Is culture alone the source of our identities? Catherine Belsey calls for a more nuanced account of what it is to be human. In the light of a characteristically lucid account of their views, as well as their debt to Kant and Hegel, she takes issue with Jean-François Lyotard, Judith Butler, and Slavoj Zizek. Drawing examples from film and art, fiction and poetry, Professor Belsey builds on the insights of her influential Critical Practice to provide not only an accessible introduction to current debates, but a major new contribution to cultural criticism and theory.

ISBN 13: 978-0-415-25288-1 (hbk)
ISBN 13: 978-0-415-25289-8 (pbk)
ISBN 13: 978-0-203-00144-8 (ebk)

Related titles from Routledge

Cultural Studies: A Critical Introduction
Simon During

Cultural Studies: A Critical Introduction is a wide-ranging and stimulating introduction to the history and theory of Cultural Studies from Leavisism, through the era of the Centre for Contemporary Cultural Studies, to the global nature of contemporary Cultural Studies.

Cultural Studies: A Critical Introduction begins with an introduction to the field and its theoretical history and then presents a series of short essays on key areas of Cultural Studies, designed to provoke discussion and raise questions. Each thematic section examines and explains a key topic within Cultural Studies.

Sections include:

- the discipline
- time
- space
- media and the public sphere
- identity
- sexuality and gender
- value

Cultural Studies: A Critical Introduction will be very useful in classrooms but will also appeal to anyone with an interest in keeping up or familiarising themselves with cultural studies in its contemporary forms.

ISBN13: 978-0-415-24656-9 (hbk)
ISBN13: 978-0-415-24657-6 (pbk)
ISBN13: 978-0-203-01758-6 (ebk)

Available at all good bookshops
For ordering and further information please visit:
www.routledge.com

The Cultural Studies Reader

Third Edition

Edited by Simon During

The Cultural Studies Reader is the ideal introduction for students to this exciting discipline. A revised introduction explaining the history and key concerns of cultural studies brings together important articles by leading thinkers to provide an essential guide to the development, key issues and future directions of cultural studies.

This fully updated third edition includes:
- 36 essays including 21 new articles
- An editor's preface succinctly introducing each article with suggestions for further reading
- Comprehensive coverage of every major cultural studies method and theory
- An updated account of recent developments in the field
- Articles on new areas such as culture and nature and the cultures of globalization
- New key thinkers such as CLR James, Gilles Deleuze, Antonio Negri and Edward Said, included for the first time
- A global appeal – *The Cultural Studies Reader* is designed to be read around the world and deals with issues relevant to each continent

Essays by: Theodor Adorno, Benedict Anderson, Arjun Appadurai, Roland Barthes, Simone de Beauvoir, Walter Benjamin, Tony Bennett, Pierre Bourdieu, Judith Butler, Michel de Certeau, Jodi Dean, Gilles Deleuze, Michel Foucault, Nancy Fraser, Paul Gilroy, Antonio Gramsci, Stuart Hall, Donna Haraway, Michael Hardt, Dick Hebdige, Max Horkheimer, C.L.R. James, Fridrich A. Kittler, Eve Kosofsky Sedgwick, Bruno Latour, Teresa de Lauretis, Henri Lefebvre, Justin Lewis, Hau Ling Cheng, Eric Ma, Meaghan Morris, Antonio Negri, Claire Parnet, Russell A. Potter, Janice A. Radway, Edward Said, Gayatri Spivak, Peter Stallybrass, Allon White, Raymond Williams.

ISBN13: 978-0-415-37412-5 (hbk)   ISBN13: 978-0-415-37413-2 (pbk)

Related titles from Routledge

Sigmund Freud

Pamela Thurschwell

Routledge Critical Thinkers series

Sigmund Freud is the ideal guide for readers wishing to explore this thinker's immense influence on contemporary culture, society and literary theory. This volume:

- outlines Freud's psychoanalytical theory and provides a clear guide to Freudian terminology
- traces the contexts and development of Freud's work over the course of his career
- explores the paradoxes and contradictions of his writing
- focuses on psychoanalysis as an interpretative strategy, paying special attention to its impact on literary and cultural theory
- examines the recent backlash against Freud and argues for the continued relevance of psychoanalysis.

The author stresses that the best way to understand Freud is to read his original texts. This guide brings those texts to life and ensures that readers of all levels will find Freud accessible, challenging and of continuing relevance.

ISBN 13: 978-0-415-21520-6 (hbk)
ISBN 13: 978-0-415-21521-3 (pbk)
ISBN 13: 978-0-203-18343-4 (ebk)

Related titles from Routledge

The Trauma Question

Roger Luckhurst

In this book Roger Luckhurst introduces and advances the fields of cultural memory and trauma studies, tracing the ways in which ideas of trauma have become a major element in contemporary Western conceptions of the self.

Luckhurst outlines the origins of the concept of trauma across psychiatric, legal and cultural-political sources, from the 1860s to the coining of Post-Traumatic Stress Disorder in 1980. He then explores the nature and extent of 'trauma culture' through English and American sources from 1980 to the present, drawing upon a range of cultural practices from literature, memoirs and confessional journalism through to photography and film. The study covers a diverse range of cultural works, from writers Toni Morrison, Stephen King and W. G. Sebald to artists like Tracey Emin, Christian Boltanski and Tracey Moffatt and film-makers David Lynch and Atom Egoyan.

The Trauma Question represents an important step forward for those seeking a greater understanding of this controversial and ever-expanding area of research.

Roger Luckhurst teaches in the School of English and Humanities, Birkbeck College, University of London. He is the author of *"The Angle Between the Walls": The Fiction of J.G. Ballard* (1997), *The Invention of Telepathy* (2002), and *Science Fiction* (2005).

ISBN13: 978-0-415-40272-9 (hbk)
ISBN13: 978-0-415- 40271-2 (pbk)

Available at all good bookshops
For ordering and further information please visit:
www.routledgeliterature.com